Using COMPUTERS in the Classroom

William L. Callison

Using Computers in the Classroom

William L. Callison

Professor of Education
California State University
at Fullerton

Prentice-Hall, Inc.   Englewood Cliffs, New Jersey 07632

Library of Congress Cataloging in Publication Data

Callison, William L.
  Using computers in the classroom.

  Bibliography:
    1. Computer-assisted instruction. 2. Education—
Computer programs—Purchasing. 3. Microcomputers—
Purchasing. I. Title.
  LB1028.5.C264 1985   371.3'9445   84-24864
  ISBN 0-13-940214-4

Cover design: Whitman Studio, Inc.
Cover photo: Courtesy of IBM Corporation
Manufacturing buyer: Barbara Kelly Kittle
Interior photographs: David Celis

Printed in the United States
10 9 8 7 6 5 4 3 2 1

ISBN   0-13-940214-4   01

Prentice-Hall International, Inc., *London*
Prentice-Hall of Australia Pty. Limited, *Sydney*
Editora Prentice-Hall do Brasil, Ltda., *Rio de Janeiro*
Prentice-Hall Canada Inc., *Toronto*
Prentice-Hall of India Private Limited, *New Delhi*
Prentice-Hall of Japan, Inc., *Tokyo*
Prentice-Hall of Southeast Asia Pte. Ltd., *Singapore*
Whitehall Books Limited, *Wellington, New Zealand*

*I am pleased to dedicate this book to my wife, **Rita**, who provided fine support, and to my students who made suggestions for its content.*

CONTENTS

FOREWORD

It is a pleasure for me to recommend this book to you as a teacher or administrator who is interested in exploring the use of microcomputers in teaching and administration. It is filled with useful suggestions that should get you off to a good start if you choose to become involved with microcomputers. It also contains some excellent reference information which I believe you will come back to again and again as you become more involved with micros and want to subscribe to a microcomputer magazine for educators, for instance.

Let me suggest that administrators and interested teachers become involved in a curriculum review with interested parties prior to the purchase of any hardware. This precludes the unhappy situation where a school may purchase a microcomputer and then, later, discover they want software that requires another machine.

Take a careful look at each subject area to see what objectives can be taught with software that is now available. Once you know what you want to teach on the micro, go out and see what software does the best job for you. Then find out what microcomputer that software runs on, and consider it for purchase.

I hope you enjoy the book. I think the suggestions make sense and I trust that use of a microcomputer will add a new dimension of richness to your teaching.

As Superintendent of a district with more than 250 microcomputers in use, I read this book for teachers and administrators with great interest and immediately decided I would like to have copies for my staff. It is clearly written and gets right to the essentials. My district is involved in extensive training of staff which will help us make good use of our many microcomputers. We are also initiating a series of evaluation studies to further understand their impact using the Concerns Based Adoption Model described in this book.

We wish you well as you learn to use this fine new technology.

Leonard Burns Ed.D.
Superintendent
Bellflower Unified School District
Bellflower, California

PREFACE

Writing this book for teachers and administrators who are interested in knowing how to start to learn about microcomputers has been a great pleasure for us. We are having a wonderful rebirth of professional interest and vigor, in part because of the new things we are learning each day about technology that can be helpful in our schools. It is important for those readers who are not ordinarily interested in technology, mathematics, physical sciences and such matters to know that the author's background is in the social sciences. We have no special predilection for technology but do have a life-long interest in approaches that can improve our teaching.

It is our interest in good teaching that has led us to explore computing and to write a book for teachers and administrators about using microcomputers to supplement instruction. The first draft of this book was written for teachers exclusively. The more we thought about it, however, the more we became convinced to write the book for both teachers and administrators.

Teachers need to know how to get started with microcomputers, and they also need the principal to understand the same things they do as they grow in sophistication. If the administrator is left behind, is not encouraged, students will suffer. Teachers will not be given full support unless they go out of their way to involve the administrator, just as they do in any other innovation they propose. This is the minimum needed for teachers to succeed. To move beyond the minimum and build a school that is a joy to work in, where students give solid academic performance, this takes something else.

A great school is constructed on the basis of mutual decision making between teachers and administrators. This means administrators must know what is really happening in classrooms and be as competent as teachers. Competent teachers know how to use technology to supplement teaching and make it interesting. The microcomputer is an important new technology. Hence, administrators need to know what teachers know about using microcomputers. At the same time, teachers need to know quite a bit about administration if decisions are to be mutual, that is, decisions among equals. Consequently, we have included some material in this book that is primarily for administrators. It is also material that teachers should know about if they, for example, want to create the best possible evaluation system to judge their work and the effect of microcomputers on that work.

We recognize that we are asking a lot of teachers. But we also know from experience that schools where excellence is visible are schools where teachers know a lot about administration. This is especially true of the evaluation process, since it is the means for directing teacher energy and bringing about improvement.

We have slowly become convinced that microcomputers are going to have a great influence on teaching in our schools. The culture of the United States is oriented to technology, which, in a sense, it must be for us to have a high standard of living. We see products that are superior to ours come on the market each month from Japan and West Germany. Therefore, it should not surprise us that their standard of living is improving more rapidly than ours. National defense pressures in the culture also cause this thrust to use and develop new and effective technology. What this means for us at the classroom level is sometimes not clear. Technologies come and go. Do you remember the language laboratories that were quite popular in the 1960's?

As we read the culture, however, we see the microcomputer having a much greater impact because it is a machine for business and home as well as the school. It is important to us because parents who see computers used in their work environment insist that their children be given experiences with microcomputers. This pressure from parents is strong, and it is becoming more persistent each year as the number of microcomputers in the society increases.

Our response to the pressure from microcomputer supporters has been varied. Initially, we did nothing because we didn't see how they could really improve instruction. The programs were just pages from workbooks. Then we heard about PLATO, which is a high-quality program. It seemed to offer intriguing interactive activities for students and we decided to find out more about it. The writer took leave from his university and went to

Vista Verde Computer Laboratory

Washington D.C. to work on a PLATO project producing software for handicapped adults.

This was both a positive and a negative experience for us. We liked all the new things we were learning about the world of computers, and we valued a chance to create software for adults who wished to work away from dependency. We disliked the boredom of writing objectives all day long, which is what some designers of software actually do.

We returned to teaching and didn't do much with computers for a while. Then we noticed how many of our students were trying to learn more about computers and decided to try to keep up with them because we want our courses to deal with the actual problems that students face each day. We began collecting materials and reading books about computers and technology once more. This book is the result of those efforts.

ACKNOWLEDGMENTS

We have been fortunate to have the assistance of several teachers who use microcomputers in their classrooms. Ms. Barbara Moore is the author of three chapters: Courseware For Elementary Teachers, Computers For The Handicapped and Administrative Applications For The Computer. She is a Vice Principal and Computer Coordinator in the Fullerton School District Fullerton, California. Ms. Moore also did the drawing in the book which is at the beginning of the Computers for the Handicapped chapter.

Mr. Roger Walden is the author of Courseware For Secondary Teachers. He is a computer using teacher in the Irvine Unified School District, Irvine, California, as is Mr. Timothy Baird who wrote the chapter Using Logo.

Mark Morrill of the Santa Ana Unified School District, Santa Ana, California wrote the training material for a non-programming inservice seen in the chapter Inservice Training for Using Microcomputers. Ms. Rondel Hardie of the Claremont Unified School District in Claremont, California and Ms. Mary Marquez of the Norwalk-La Mirada Unified School District in Norwalk, California gathered information for the chapter Using Computers in the Community College.

David Celis and several of his students at the Vista Verde School in the Irvine Unified School District provided the photographs with the support of Principal Barbara Barnes.

CHAPTER ONE
COMPUTERS IN THE CLASSROOM

Some teachers have a natural interest in machines and technology that helps them lead the movement to utilize microcomputers for instruction in our schools. Most of us in education are drawn to the micro through a different process, however. We are professionals and we explore whatever avenues seem promising as means for improving instruction.

The objectives of this book focus on improving instruction. They are to:

1. Help teachers and administrators become aware of the possibilities for improving instruction through the use of **microcomputers** (definitions of technical terms will be found in the Glossary at the end of the book; technical terms will be in bold face type) in classrooms and laboratories;

2. Provide teachers and administrators with background that will facilitate the purchase and use of microcomputers by providing information in key areas such as **computer-assisted instruction (CAI)**, selection of **courseware** and **hardware**, model programs, and listings of computer magazines and catalogs; and

3. To encourage administrators to learn the same things teachers need to know in order to use microcomputers and to supplement this with increased understanding of competencies in planning, evaluation and the change process.

Administrators need "hands on" understanding of microcomputers in order to carefully guide teachers to successful experiences with them. This means the administrators will need to learn first from the teachers who know the most and then plan individualized strategies to involve reluctant teachers.

The chapters "Helping Yourself to Change," "A Planning Approach for Introducing Microcomputers", "Using Computers in the Community College" and "How Much Are Teachers Using the Micros?" are especially appropriate for administrators although many teachers will also be interested.

This book focuses on the use of microcomputers because it is oriented to teachers and instruction. These are the small "home" computers that teachers are introducing into their classrooms. **Mini** or medium sized "stand alone" **computers** and **mainframe** or large "time-sharing" computers are used primarily by administrators at the district office level for administrative purposes. Some large districts find it financially advantageous to use mainframe computers to deliver instruction through **terminals** in classrooms and laboratories as well. The use of PLATO in this way is discussed in Chapter 4.

As you begin your search for information about microcomputers, keep in mind that some areas of the school curriculum have obvious tasks where microcomputers can be used. These are the drill and practice aspects of mathematics, business and vocational education. Hence, look first in these areas to find out which teachers know the most and may be willing to help you. In some schools this has been particularly true of the math teachers. They have learned so much, so fast that they think of computing as an aspect of their math activities. Other teachers are sometimes hesitant to get involved when this is the case.

We should probably encourage teachers from social studies or the humanities to be in charge of computer facilities and let the math teachers work with them as consultants in order to reach the most faculty who may learn to supplement instruction with microcomputer courseware. We believe, on the basis of our work in developing computer courseware, that the teachers from the humanities will dominate the field of courseware creation in the future. Good computer instruction finally gets down to the ability of the designer to create imaginative interactions between the student and the program of courseware.

The books on computers we have read indicate the most widespread application of the computer in our time will be its use as a **word processor**. Your friendly, local English teacher may be surprised to find out she is going to be at the center of these developments.

You may have guessed that we are very encouraged by the data indicating how computers can enhance instruction. Let's turn to some of that data for a moment. Peter Rizza reports that in twelve **computer-managed instruction** (CMI) PLATO projects across the country, students are achieving one year of growth in reading by spending from 12 to 30 hours at the terminal. (1)

The Chicago City Schools Project, begun in 1971, involves some 12,000 students from fourth through eighth grade. These are primarily inner-city children using 850 terminals providing tutorial lessons in mathematics and reading. Prior to the Project, the average increase in reading ability was 5.4 months per pupil for each 10 months of regular instruction. Project students, on the other hand, are averaging 9.0 months gain for 8 months of instruction.(2)

Overall, a review of the literature reveals the following consistencies:

1. The use of computer assisted instruction (CAI) either improved learning or showed no differences when compared to the traditional classroom approach.(3)
2. The use of CAI reduced learning time when compared to the regular classroom.(4)
3. The use of CAI improved student attitudes toward the use of computers in the learning situation.(5)
4. The development of CAI courseware following specified guidelines can result in portability and their acceptance and use by other faculty.(6)

Indeed, teachers all over the country are using whatever resources they have to purchase microcomputers for their classrooms. In 1985 we have more than 500,000 (7) micros in our schools, even during a time when school resources are meager.

Computer Assisted Instruction in Language

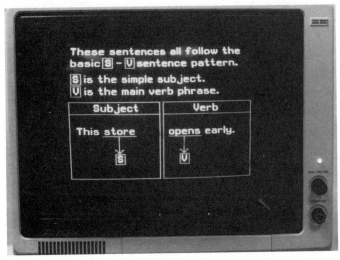

Many of us who have been involved in the educational use of computers believe that the chief limiting factor at the moment is not lack of money to purchase hardware, but, rather, a lack of quality **software** (the programs that one puts in the machines). When software is designed to teach, we call it courseware. Courseware is an important concern in this book, and we will explore various characteristics of the educational courseware available. Before doing this, however, we will provide some background about educational computing in general.

CHAPTER TWO
BACKGROUND

The history of computers is a story focusing on making computers more widely available and easier to use. The first computer was probably the **abacus.** In the 1600's Pascal developed a calculator that could add and subtract, and Hollerith created an electric data tabulator to compute the 1890 census in the US. During the late 1930's and 1940's great progress was made in the US and Europe. The first **vacuum-tube computer** was developed at the University of Pennsylvania during World War II to determine missile trajectories and predict the weather. The invention of the **transistor** in 1948 made modern computers practical because of their dependability, small size and low power requirements.

The first generation of computers were manufactured in the period 1953-60, and included the Univac I, IBM 704, RCA Bizmac, and the Honeywell D-1000. The second generation computers (1959 through the early 1960's) used transistors instead of vacuum tubes. Third generation computers use **microchips** and other forms of miniaturization. There is considerable debate over the nature of a fourth generation and whether it has arrived.

In the 1950's programming languages such as **FORTRAN** and **COBOL** were developed. In the mid 1960's Kemeny and Kurtz at Dartmouth created **BASIC**, the language teachers usually learn and teach their students (sometimes their students teach them).

The idea of computer literacy for the general student population emerged in the 1960's. The Conference Board of the Mathematical Sciences, in its 1972 report, (8) recommended universal computer literacy, suggesting it be taught in the junior high schools.

Computers can be useful to students as an aid to learning in the tutor ("teacher") mode where the student directs the action by programming the computer. Use of the word processor is another example of the tutor mode where writing can be typed, edited, stored and corrected for spelling errors. Students are now having tutee experiences in geometry, art and music. Both tutor and tutee modes are valuable and their use should depend upon the educational objective the teacher is teaching to.

Computers are also used in problem solving, as in the use of DIALOG for literature searches. DIALOG is a system available to teachers; through their classroom micro they can enter the ERIC system (which catalogs published and unpublished materials in education) and many other data bases.

If you think about how hand calculators are changing the teaching of math, imagine how hand held microcomputers will impact math and other areas of curriculum. This day is upon us as the first pamphlet sized micro is now on the market for about $100.

In addition to assisting in learning and problem solving, computers and information science are the subject of study and an important new discipline.

> Microelectronics has been the key to improved performance and decreased costs . . . responsiveness to human needs has become the primary challenge facing system designers. How well the industry fulfills this goal will determine whether the emerging information services of the 1980's realize their potential both for improving the quality of life and achieving much needed productivity gains.(9)

Computer programmers continue to be in great demand with 35% more jobs available this year than last and computing power growing at 40% per year.(10) Preparation for these opportunities begins at the elementary school level. Seymour Papert at the Massachusetts Institute of Technology has created a special programming language for children called LOGO (see Chapter 11). When LOGO is turned on, a pointed arrow called a "turtle" is displayed and can be moved about the screen to draw objects of interest to the child. This allows the child to control activities in the tutor mode. This capability is then used to involve the child in actively solving a series of problems. It is fun to imagine the many ways that a language like LOGO can be used to improve elementary school instruction. LOGO also teaches the child to think logically and to carefully follow intellectual rules and procedures. These are critical competencies in an information oriented society.

CHAPTER THREE
HOW TO GET INVOLVED

There are a variety of issues for teachers to address as they begin to work with microcomputers. These include:

1. Achievement: Learn how to help students achieve more in a shorter time. High quality programs like PLATO, the reading approach mentioned at the beginning of this chapter, already can accomplish this objective. PLATO programs have been available only for large computers until recently. Now they are becoming available for micros on a program by program basis as they are adapted for the smaller computers. As other high quality courseware (such as the Milliken math series) becomes available for micros, we will see more impressive achievement.

2. Cost reduction: Reduce costs in areas such as bilingual education, business and mathematics. Any instructional area were there is a need for drill and practice is an ideal place to utilize micros with their never-ceasing patience and reliability.

3. Increasing program stability: Make changes which will have a lasting impact. This may be especially appealing to teachers who are tired of having programs discontinued before complete data on their effectiveness is gathered and studied. Because of the significant cost of technology and the difficulties involved in introducing it to an organization, it will tend to become rather permanent once it is established. This will be especially true when it makes teachers' work easier and more successful.

4. Prepare for change: Prepare for massive change that is coming even if teachers resist it. Parents with business and professional backgrounds and students are pushing for the introduction of microcomputers. Parents see how important the technology is in job advancement and students like the machines because they are more interesting than much that goes on in school.

5. Influence curriculum: Influence curriculum as it is being developed. Teachers now have a good deal of influence over textbook selection because they understand books and the system through which they are chosen. They need to develop the same capability in order to have impact on the computer courseware that is being developed. This will require an understanding of what they can demand in a set of courseware. At the moment their passive role gives them almost no influence and so individuals who develop courseware do so with profit rather than educational quality as the main criterion. This will change only when teachers learn what they want and insist on it through the adoption process. This will also require reversal of the present practice where a school district quickly purchases hardware because of community pressure. Then staff start to look for software that runs on the micro they bought. Finally they may ask the question "How does this relate to our district approved curriculum?" We suggest just the opposite be the practice.

The district should develop a Master Plan for Computer Utilization. This should include a review of the existing curriculum to identify courses with objectives that can be taught with existing courseware. Then staff should preview courseware, and study the programs that teach what they need. Once they find the programs they like, then they can decide on the micros that will run the programs. This can save thousands of dollars. Some districts first bought hardware and then discovered too late it would not run the programs they wanted for their students.

Of these opportunities for involvement we find the two most compelling to be the need to influence curriculum and the permanence of technological change. We must slow down and go through a process much like textbook adoption in selecting courseware. The rapid change of curricula before its usefulness has been thoroughly tested is one of the most destructive characteristics of our schools. Computer courseware should, by its nature, force us to study its effectiveness at length prior to any move to discontinue it. It is just too expensive to make casual decisions about it. This

First Courseware, Then Hardware

is especially true of the high quality courseware which costs much more than the programs created "on my Apple at home" do.

As teachers learn more about courseware, they will insist on high quality products that include not only computer activities, but films, video tapes, slides, games, simulations and print materials as well, as part of the instructional materials. These high quality products will eventually drive the "quickie" materials off the market. In the meantime we can expect to hear teachers who have bought the inexpensive courseware complain that it is boring to students and that therefore they don't believe in using micros for instruction.

There are also subject matter differences in the quality of courseware at the present. Math and science teachers tend to have developed a concensus about what should be taught in their areas, and this leads to the possibility of effective courseware development. In the language arts, the situation is reversed, and the courseware is not impressive in many cases.

CHAPTER FOUR
COMPUTER-ASSISTED INSTRUCTION

We use the heading CAI here because it is familiar to teachers. When this technology is used, all instruction is delivered utilizing the computer. **Drill and Practice** programs are used when teachers are working on skill development in reading, mathematics, spelling and foreign languages. They need to be used sparingly because they can become boring. Some uninformed teachers see one of these programs and condemn all CAI as boring. Tutorial programs instruct the student just as the teacher would in a one-on-one situation. The student responds to questions by typing in responses the program has been prepared to anticipate. It is fun to create these programs if one is good at thinking of all the possible responses students may come up with.

Demonstration and simulation programs are commonly connected with the teaching of science, although they can be used with good effect in other subject areas as well. This is especially true if the computer you buy has good graphics capabilities. Many of the things you now would use an overhead projector for can be done even better using graphics on a computer.

Simulation programs are built around real or imaginary models and are very exciting for students. We worked on a simulated model where a handicapped adult had to cope with a land-lord who did not want to abide by the city code requiring that a ramp be built when an apartment is rented to a person who uses a wheel chair. The simulation involved the student in a great variety of planning and political activities of the type needed in real life in dealing with such problems. This is exciting material for students.

Educational activities using a game format are another form of CAI and they can be effective supplements to instruction. They require students to use sets of rules which may be quite complex. Preview CAI programs before you purchase them to make sure they are at the right level for your students. Do you remember getting in a hurry and not proof-reading a dittoed test for students? The same disastrous results can occur if you don't preview microcomputer programs. Because your school has invested a large sum of money in the program, you may end up even more embarrassed than you were with the "typos" on the test.

It is helpful to keep in mind the dual use of many of the so-called "tools" used in the microcomputer world. The word processor programs are our favorite, as they will be for almost anyone at your school who types a good deal. They can be used to teach students to outline material, to write to the outline, and to make editing revisions. Even those persons who don't like to type seem to enjoy using the word processor. Perhaps the difference is in the ease with which corrections can be made before material is printed on a page.

Another tool which can be widely used for instruction is your numeric analysis program. The most common one is called VisiCalc, which is described in Chapter 15, and there are others that are similar. Any class where numbers are used, including social studies classes, can make exciting use of a numeric program.

Data processing programs offer instructional opportunities in classes where large amounts of data can be gathered and analyzed; for example, in a US Government class which is conducting a community survey.

The next step beyond CAI technologically is Computer-Based Testing (CBT). There are two types of CBT. In the first, all test results are used for administrative purposes, as in a state required test, and may not be shared with teachers in certain situations. More helpful to teachers is the type where the results are reported to teachers to assist them in developing appropriate curricula for their students.

The step after CBT is Computer-Managed Instruction (CMI). There are at least five types of CMI at this time. In type one, student responses to a test are placed on computer cards and read by a scanner. The information is then sent on to the computer which is programmed to give recommendations based on criteria built into the program. In type two, the student takes the test on the computer which in turn calculates the result immediately and informs the student which answers were correct. Some programs of this type then place the student in a program to work on the areas of deficiency.

In types three and four there is no testing; they are record-keeping programs. They are distinguished by the amount of information that is stored. In type three, information pertaining to a specific content area is stored, while in type four, extensive information across all subject areas is stored for purposes such as report card preparation.

The fifth type is a powerful technology such as that seen in the PLATO programs. A given module typically includes 60% CAI and 40% non-computer instruction delivered through video tapes, films, slides, audio tapes and print materials. This variety in instructional delivery approaches makes the material even more interesting than CAI, a fine way to learn in its own right. The power of what we might call "Multi-Sensory CMI" then, is two fold: it is individualized and it uses the most appropriate media to present a given type of material.

In the author's experience developing PLATO courseware for special education students, we frequently introduced a 30-minute module with a 5-minute video tape sequence giving the student a visual picture of the module content. We might then have a 15-minute CAI segment of sequential instruction on the topic. This could be followed by 5 minutes of still pictures in the form of slides showing key examples of articles or equipment related to the content. We could then close the module with 5 minutes of drill and practice on CAI.

PLATO SCHOOLS CAN AFFORD

Dr. Pamela Wright, consultant to California State University at Sacramento and to the State University System as a whole has recently written the following description of a new use of PLATO with important implications for schools.

In September, 1983, Chaffey (California) Joint Union School District introduced a new dimension to its Alternative Studies Program aimed at retrieving the truant/dropout population. The Alternative Studies Program utilizes PLATO which is leased through the State Univesity System. The State of California provides an average of $2000 per year to support this type of student, and the District needs approximately 35 students to attend five minimum days of instruction per week to get its full payment per student.

PLATO has been highly successful with this particular student population and by uniting Independent Study with PLATO it is possible to provide a full academic program. Since PLATO can provide a continuum of curriculum which both integrates and matches the District adopted objective based curriculum, it makes it possible to enroll a student in the courses required for a high school diploma and have all the requirements met on the computer. The PLATO system evaluates the student for proper placement in the diagnostic and prescriptive application. The management system notes each time a student accesses the terminal and records everything the student does, so that all the tracking is completed at the same time an audit trail is being provided. As a student proceeds, s(he) is continuously assessed in order to provide the proper flow through the curricula.

The curricula is not only objective based, but it is mastery based learning, guaranteeing that the material is completely understood before the student progresses. Students are highly motivated and there has never been a need to recruit students. Approximately 100 students have been enrolled in the PLATO Learning Center and without exception PLATO is the most attractive and successful aspect of the entire Independent Study Program.

PLATO not only has the capability of providing required courses for credit but it can also prepare students for the high school equivalency examination. PLATO also provides college courses for credit as well as a vast amount of vocational training.

This system also offers the opportunity to generate revenue by reaching adults who take credit courses through Adult Education. Additionally, revenue may be generated by subletting terminals (there are eight in the PLATO Learning Center) to the Regional Opportunity Program (vocational education), local industry and colleges in the area. These funds allow the Learning Center to pay for itself and even support instruction for regular students who are not included in the revenue generating categories mentioned above.

Currently there is a class of advanced high school students who use PLATO terminals in the morning from 6:30 to 7:30 AM for the purpose of taking courses that would otherwise not be available. In the evening Adult Education students use the terminals to prepare for the high school equivalency examination as well as to take a reading course.

There are numerous studies available to validate student progress on PLATO. On the average, students will progress approximately one grade level per subject for every 20 to 30 hours on the system. The greatest improvements are seen with high school and adult students who are performing below grade level expectations. PLATO is also used to assist students who fail the District (State required) proficiency examination by providing remediation.

The District has had many visitors and other districts are now taking advantage of this opportunity which was made possible when the State University System purchased PLATO from Control Data Corporation (CDC). These PLATO programs were developed using the University of Illinois quality control requirements, including extensive field-testing of materials in classrooms. They were consequently expensive to develop. Perhaps we should refer to them as Illinois-PLATO to distinguish them from a newer set of materials, also owned by CDC, which we could call micro-PLATO. Dr. Wright has reviewed both types of PLATO material and suggested to the author in a telephone interview that Illinois-PLATO is superior to any courseware on the market, while micro-PLATO may be as good as 80% of the courseware on the market.

At the national level, then, CDC has the following micro-PLATO programs available for the Texas Instruments 99/4A microcomputer:

Basic Mathematics   Includes courses in basic number concepts, basic arithmetic operations plus special applications in ratio, proportion, percent and geometry measurement.

Basic Reading   Covers basic fundamentals of word structure, fundamental vocabulary and basic comprehension skills.

Basic Grammar   Features basic language structure and word usage, sentence and paragraph structure and mechanics and conventions on writing.

High School Math   Includes algebra and geometry concepts as well as the practical applications of arithmetic. Drill and practice and tutorial lessons help students understand averages, measurements, data interpretation and real numbers.

High School Reading   Provides exercises in practical reading, including understanding instructions, contracts, library references and newspapers.

High School Writing   Emphasizes grammar skills, spelling, punctuation, capitalization, sentence structure, logic and organization.

Social Studies   Includes economics, geography, political science, history and behavioral science.

High School Science   Includes biology, earth science, chemistry and physics.

Of these offerings, Basic Math and High School Math will be available for the IBM PC soon. Courseware for the Apple ll Plus and the Apple lle includes Algebra (for use with such texts as Holt Algebra 1, Algebra Structure and Method, Algebra, HBJ Algebra 1 and Merrill Algebra), Foreign Languages, Computer Literacy and Personal Development.

Computer based education is a powerful force that can provide extensive benefits when used in a carefully planned manner.

Benefits of CAI

The Irvine Unified School District in Irvine, California has created a list of benefits teachers can derive from using CAI.

Instruction

Computers are suitable for students of all achievement levels.

Computers are suitable to and effective with both individual and small group learners. They provide individualized, self-paced instruction.

Computers enhance a student-centered curriculum.

Computers offer excellent adaptation to the special needs of handicapped students.

CAI can provide enrichment activities for students at all achievement levels.

CAI can upgrade student performance, showing gains in both cognitive and affective domains.

CAI can be motivating, especially for underachievers.

Computers can relieve the burden of drill and practice, make-up lessons, and review.

Computers can help the teacher diagnose areas of student weaknesses.

CAI provides immediate feedback.

Computers allow application of proven teaching methods to all students at all times because the computer does not discriminate on the basis of personality, background, or the previous day's behavior.

Computer programs can offer challenging logic and simulation activities. Programs can also assist with spatial relationships, where girls frequently do not do well.

Word processing programs encourage student writing skills in English classes.

Program and Record Keeping Management

Tests can be generated by the computer. Teachers can program tests themselves, or use an **authoring language** system.

Teacher-made and standardized tests can be scored and results kept in convenient files for future reference. Computers can analyze test data for diagnosis and prescription purposes.

Programmed gradebook programs allow easy recordkeeping of student grades.

Word processing programs are useful in correspondence, such as letters to parents. Mailing lists for groups such as parents may be used over again.

Computer programs can determine reading levels of text materials.

Although this is not an exhaustive list, it does give one some specific ideas about the many ways a computer can assist teachers in the classroom.

We turn now to the consideration of four approaches capable of delivering CMI, the technology where computer-assisted instruction is supplemented by film, video tape, slides and print materials. One of these, TICCIT, is still too expensive for most school systems.

Illinois-PLATO, as we have indicated, is important because it has by far the largest number of courses available for instructional use and they are high quality courses.

TICCIT is intriguing because it is designed for school people and other users who wish to program their own courses.

TRS 80 is the number one selling microcomputer and has impressive capabilities, including over 20 hours of free training for teachers.

APPLE II/IIe is the microcomputer most widely purchased in schools thus far and it has the most extensive courseware.

Several other systems, including Atari, PET, IBM and Texas Instruments are also widely used in schools and each has advantages and disadvantages, depending upon one's needs.

Apple IIe System

There are three sizes of computer hardware. Mainframe or time-sharing computers are large, require expensive telephone connections to classroom terminals and can do things like store large amounts of student test information and process it rapidly. Individual schools probably don't need one of these unless they are going to use the mainframe for delivering instruction, which some large districts do. District offices usually have a mainframe to handle payroll, accounting and other tasks where large amounts of information need to be stored.

The minicomputer "stands alone"; that is, it is not connected to a central system but offers a medium amount of memory and storage capacity. Schools can perform many tasks in addition to instruction with a mini, including attendance and grade reporting. TICCIT utilizes a minicomputer.

The microcomputer is the one everyone is talking about and is the focus of this book. It is small, like a little television set connected to a typewriter, and it is inexpensive. It has a small but impressive memory and is selling at the rate of about 300,000 a year. We expect to have 500,000 in US schools alone in 1985.

Illinois-PLATO offers the most courses or courseware, about 3,000 hours or the equivalent of 55 school courses which meet five days a week for 45 minutes a day.

Basic Skills, Illinois-Plato's biggest selling set of CMI courses, utilizes a variety of media including CAI (60 to 75%), text and video tape. We mention it often here because we see it as a model teachers should suggest when they get the opportunity to influence the type of programs that should supplement state adopted texts. It is:

Individualized, providing immediate feedback to each student based upon her or his responses. Learners are helped to select the pathway through material which is most appropriate for their needs.

Modular in structure, with instruction presented in small, well-defined units which are less intimidating than large blocks of material.

Objective-based, with competencies students are expected to acquire in terms of learning outcomes. Students begin with simple objectives and move to more complex material as they grow more confident.

Based on the mastery learning model, where each objective must be achieved before the student moves to further material.

Diagnostic and prescriptive in that each student is assessed at the beginning of instruction to identify skill deficiencies. This information is then used to direct the student to material appropriate for his or her needs.

Multi-sensory in format in that it uses the media mentioned previously. The CAI portion is interactive so the learners respond either by typing on a keyboard or touching the flexible terminal screen which displays text, graphics, and animation.

Uses a variety of instructional approaches including tutorial lessons, drill and practice lessons, remedial help sequences, review and practice activities, and diagnostic, mastery and retention tests.

In addition to the materials already mentioned, the student has textual overviews, exercise manuals, and application activities.

Other CMI programs designed for microcomputers offer many of these features. TICCIT, which uses a minicomputer, also provides terminal displays in color with all visual media including film, videotape, and slides seen on the terminal screen rather than in other parts of the room, as is the case with Illinois-PLATO. TICCIT offers training for school districts to prepare staff to develop their own courseware.

Vendors selling microcomputers typically do not offer much, if any, courseware. The possibility that school districts can begin to develop their own courseware is appealing, but in the beginning it is likely to be what is called Level 1, mainly drill and practice exercises.

To make material more interesting to students, greater expertise and expense is required in courseware development. The potential cost of courseware development should be considered when computer hardware is being analyzed, because in the long run the courseware is more expensive. A team of four courseware developers may take one month to develop one hour of courseware at a cost of $ 10,000 per month. Thus, a typical high school course could cost $550,000 to develop.

The advantage to schools in developing their own courseware is the acquisition of a product that exactly meets their requirements. The disadvantages are the cost and the difficulty in finding staff who enjoy this solitary, non-teacher-like activity. Perhaps if school districts joined together in networks, they could create courseware, utilizing programmers from the local community college or high school students when they can do the job.

As we mentioned earlier, Illinois-PLATO is expensive. An Illinois-PLATO terminal costs approximately $5000 for hardware and $950 per month in subscription and communication costs. Hence, few school districts have purchased Illinois-PLATO. Now that the "drop-out" model is getting attention, there should be a strong response from schools.

TICCIT runs with a minimum of four terminals and it costs $125,000. Since it is a "stand alone" system, it has a minimum of communication costs.

The microcomputers are not as expensive in terms of hardware, but they offer relatively less in instructional quality. The Apple IIe for example, costs around $1900 for 64,000 (K) of memory. This means when the computer is turned off, the material it has been processing is erased. If one wishes to retain the material, it is stored on a "floppy disk" which is like a small, 45 RPM record. To use Apple IIe, one also needs a disk drive with controller for about $400 and a color monitor for about $300. Thus the cost of the system is about $1600. An Apple system can be used for student instruction, b) research and data collection, and c) classroom management (of objectives achieved and curriculum developed.)

The TRS 80, made by Radio Shack, costs about $500 for 16,000 characters of memory. If a school wishes to coordinate instruction across 16

Getting an Early Start on Computer Literacy

terminals, a network controller may be purchased for an additional $300. If the courseware were available, this low-cost system might dominate school use as it now does home use.

As educators we are faced with a dilemma. The expensive systems like Illinois-PLATO and TICCIT offer very fine CMI, including a variety of supporting media to make the instruction interesting and effective. The systems that are affordable have a more limited capability, and we need to choose carefully to find courseware that will not bore students.

As we have indicated, computers used in instruction increase the modes or types of instruction. These include drill and practice, games, programming practice, problem solving, simulations, tutorials and combinations of the above. To be instructionally "literate" a teacher should be able to use each of these techniques to enhance learning. Computer literacy for teachers is a knowledge of computers and their applications as they affect students and the rest of society. This literacy should be at the same level of knowledge and skill an individual is mastering in other aspects of her/his life.

CHAPTER FIVE
A MODEL PROGRAM

The Alessandro Middle School in the Moreno Valley Unified School District in Sunnymead, California, is an active center of microcomputer use. The Title I Reading and Math Lab is the center of the action and it is directed by Ms. Mary Bruce. It provides us with an interesting model for making inservice training available to teachers and administrators from the district.

Alessandro School utilizes 10 Apple II/IIe computers to provide participating students with multilevel computer assisted instruction through drill and practice exercises in both reading/language arts and math concepts.

The purpose of the lab is to provide a diagnostic/prescriptive program in reading, language arts and math to meet the diagnosed needs of Title I students based on the reading, language arts, writing and math sections of the District's Competency Based Education (CBE) test.

To provide drill and practice program help to participating students to improve their test scores in all basic skill areas on district-adopted and other tests of reference.

To offer alternative modes of teaching techniques and materials for participating students.

The scope of inservice provided by the lab for district teachers and administrators is as follows:

a. Computer literacy
b. How computers can revolutionize teaching techniques
c. Software demonstration
d. Apple Writer and its uses (a word processor program)
e. VisiCalc and its uses (a computation program)
f. Computer-assisted attendance reporting
g. Computer-assisted grade reporting

This lab assists teachers in learning to utilize the computer in their own teaching situation. It further offers them an opportunity to view software (courseware) of interest, which is a great service, since some publishers will not let potential purchasers view materials before purchase. Too many people have copied the courseware and then returned it without paying for it. The lab offers teachers a fine chance to see examples of two widely selling programs. Apple Writer is an excellent example of a word processing program, and VisiCalc is the best selling single software program in the nation. Finally, the lab offers help to administrators in demonstrating practical programs for attendance and grade reporting.

CHAPTER SIX
SELECTING COURSEWARE AND HARDWARE FOR YOUR SCHOOL

A. Courseware

Although most school people are now indicating one should locate appropriate courseware before selecting a microcomputer, we still hear of contrary examples. As we learn more about utilization of micros we would suggest a series of steps that should precede hardware selection.

At this point in planning to purchase courseware and hardware you may suggest a review of curriculum objectives to see what existing courseware may be appropriate for supplementing your present curriculum. It is very important for your staff that will be involved in courseware selection to work closely with the district curriculum committee(s). This will allow you to integrate courseware into the curriculum in an orderly fashion, and, at the same time, underscore the district's serious intent to use microcomputers as a regular part of curricula as good courseware becomes available.

Computer-oriented people classify courseware as part of software. Thus a list of software for your district would include all the courseware plus programs that you can think of as tools to accomplish certain types of tasks. Examples of tools might include word processing programs at several levels of sophistication such as Apple Writer II and WordStar. The most common numeric analysis software is VisiCalc. Sometimes computer people use the term software, which is more commonly known to the lay public, when they mean courseware. This is done to make the material seem more comfortable to individuals who are just getting started using computers.

The following article, "How to Be a Software Whiz," based on materials from the Northwest Regional Educational Laboratory and published in the March, 1982, issue of The Executive Educator illustrates this usage.(11)

For schools to have microcomputers without satisfactory software is a little like having a telephone without knowing anybody's number: the equipment itself is marvelous, but unless you're blessed by blind, dumb luck, using it won't get you the time of day.

Trouble is, hundreds of firms—from multinationals to enterprising dolts in some garage—are offering software packages to schools and the trick, as usual, is buying wisely.

To help school officials evaluate the microcomputer software now available, the Northwest Regional Educational Laboratory (NWREL) in Portland, Oregon, established **MicroSift** (Microcomputer Software and Information for Teachers), a clearinghouse devoted to developing and disseminating information about microcomputer software. With a grant from the National Institute of Education, NWREL has devised a model evaluation process to enable curriculum specialists new to computer education—as well as educators familiar with the field—to judge micro-computer software properly. The 25 items listed here explain the 25 evaluation criteria listed on the form seen in the Courseware Evaluation Chapter. With this form and the more detailed information, guidelines, and suggestions in hand, you should be able to make an excellent evaluation of virtually any microcomputer software package.

All of the information that follows including the Courseware Evaluation and Courseware Description forms comes from MicroSift's **Evaluator's Guide**, which the School of Education at the University of Oregon recently published. NWREL publishes reviews of specific microcomputer software packages in a quarterly newsletter, **MicroSIFT News**. To receive **MicroSIFT News**, and for further information about NWREL's activities, write to NWREL, 300 S.W. Sixth Avenue, Portland, Oregon, 97204.

To obtain the **Evaluator's Guide**, simply request it from any collection of ERIC (Educational Resources Information Center) microfiche at university libraries, state education departments, or ICCE, 135 Education, University of Oregon, Eugene, Oregon 97403. ERIC also plans to publish MicroSIFT's software reviews. Meanwhile, here's a condensed version of the guide's main elements:

Content

1. The content is accurate.   Make sure that the information and the instructional approach is not out of date and that no factual errors exist. If the software uses simulation (for a science experiment, for example), be sure that any models or examples are valid and not over-simplified. Be sure statistics and displays are accurate.

2. The content has educational value.   You'll have to use your own criteria to determine whether a specific item of courseware is educational, but here's some help: A. The content and objectives of the software should be addressed in your school's curriculum. B. The knowledge and skills the software teaches should have some utility in some aspect of life. C. The package should be useful in a specific instructional situation. D. Use of the package should enable you to learn something about curricular needs of the students. E. The content of the package should be central to the subject you are teaching.

3. The content is free of racial, ethnic, and sex stereotypes.   Make sure no racial, ethnic, or sex groups are overrepresented at the expense of others, and be certain these groups are not portrayed in terms that are indicative of false generalizations about the characteristics of the group.

Instructional Quality

4. The purpose of the package is well defined.   Usually, you'll find the purposes, goals, or objectives listed in materials that accompany the software package. The objectives should be explicit, succinct, and free of jargon. The package should include both general and specific statements of purpose; that is, the overall purpose of the package should be stated concisely, and specific objectives should be listed for specific components.

5. The package achieves its defined purpose.   Software may be evaluated in much the same way other instructional materials are evaluated—starting with instructional objectives. Based on these objectives, students should learn what the material sets out to teach, rather than merely engage in the process that the computer demands. The best way to tell if a software package achieves its objectives is by observing a student conduct a sample run of the program.

6. Presentation of the content is clear and logical.   How are terms, facts, concepts, and principles presented? The information should be well organized. The structure of the program should be evident from the outset. Definitions and explanations should be available when necessary—either in the program itself or in the support materials. The progression of the presentation should be logical and well identified. Examples and illustrations should be used where possible and should be relevant to what you want taught.

7. The level of difficulty is appropriate for the target audience. Several concerns are important here: A. The means of response (multiple choice, manipulatable graphics, single keystroke, for example) must be appropriate for the grade level of the students who will use the program. B. Students must be able to read and understand the support materials and program text; vocabulary, phrasing, and sentence length are important considerations. C. Examples and graphic illustrations must be suitable for the ability of students. D. The time required for a student to complete the program should not exceed the attention span of the typical student. E. The size and number of steps in logical processes must be suitable for the ability of students. F. The program should branch automatically to easier problems for students who are having trouble or to more difficult problems for those students who have mastered easier problems.

8. Graphics, sound and color are used for appropriate instructional reasons. These techniques should enhance, not detract from, the instructional process. Sound should not disturb others in class. Graphics, sound and color should focus attention on important content areas and should stimulate student interest.

9. Use of the package is motivational. Students should have a positive attitude about the software program. To make that happen, the program should address students in a conversational, personal style. The tone should be warm, friendly, helpful, even humorous. Students should be able to respond—and the program should respond—in a variety of ways. To ensure that students want to use the program again, reinforcement must be positive and dignified.

10. The package effectively challenges student creativity. Students should play an active, rather than passive, role at the computer. In other words, the program should allow the students to make as many decisions as possible and should be designed to anticipate a wide range of responses. In most subject areas, it's well to look for programs that provide open-ended questions with no 'right' or 'wrong' answers and that give students information to judge their own responses. The package should challenge students to think creatively and should suggest areas for further exploration.

11. Feedback on student responses is effectively employed. For feedback to be credible to students, it must be relevant to their responses. It should tell why a response was incorrect and should assess the concept being taught, not merely its form. (For example, word order might be more important than content in a certain exercise.) Feedback should be non-threatening and should occur immediately after a response. It should give cues, hints, and explanations and should adapt to each student by adjusting the level of difficulty of the content. Finally, the program might tally the percentage of correct problems out of the total number the student attempts.

12. The learner controls the rate and sequence of presentations and reviews.   Students should be able to control the amount of time needed to solve a problem or to read display material. The program should allow them to begin at a point appropriate to past achievement and not necessarily lock students into a specific instructional sequence. Students should be able to review instructions or to ask for 'help,' 'hint,' or 'dictionary' by pushing a key.

13. Instruction is integrated with previous student experiences.   The program should be designed to take into account the background of the target audience. For example, some students might better understand liquid metric measurements within the context of filling a car with gasoline rather than filling a graduated cylinder with water. Known situations should be used to explain unfamiliar situations; instruction should move from concrete to the abstract, the simple to the complicated, the familiar to the unfamiliar.

14. Learning may be extended to different situations.   Not only must the program prepare students for the next unit in the software package, but it also must enable them to use the lessons acquired at the computer in 'real life' situations away from the computer.

Technical Quality

15. User support materials are comprehensive.   Good support materials come in many forms, but you must be able to assess their value for teachers and students. **Student materials**: The package should contain preinstruction activities relating to the program, a guide to use the package, follow-up activities to reinforce instruction, and worksheets. **Teacher information**: The package should include a description of the instructional activity, suggestions about how best to use the hardware (whether to use the computer in a classroom, in small groups, in a resource center), prerequisite skills students and teachers should have, and instructions for preinstructional and post–instructional activities. **Resource information**: The package should contain a bibliography of resource information related to the content of the program, possibilities for modification, and descriptions of any models used in simulations. **Technical documentation**: Look for a detailed explanation of how to operate the program. This should include a list of special codes, instructions on how to interpret 'error' messages you might see on the computer screen, flowcharts or diagrams of the program, and an explanation of any other extraordinary features of the package. **Containers**: The package should include folders or binders for storing printed material, disks, cassettes, or other materials as well as a box or other container for organizing and storing the entire package.

16. User support materials are effective.   It's fairly easy to tell if the support materials are effective, although you must consider many factors. The materials should be attractive and durable. The text, pictures, and graphics should be clear, readable, and appropriate for the grade level of the students. You should be able to store the package easily, yet protecting the package and gaining access to the materials should not pose a problem. Students should be able to use the support material on a table typically found near a microcomputer station.

17. Information displays are effective.   Again, you have many factors to consider here, but determining whether the information displayed on the computer screen is effective is fairly straightforward. Graphic displays should not be too complex or too full of information. The same goes for textual information. It should be clear, unambiguous, not too long, and easy to read. There should be an appropriate mix of graphics and text, and the transitions should be smooth and unobtrusive. Text position should be consistent or predictable so students don't have to hunt for the information.

18. Students can operate the program easily and independently. Without good and accurate directions, students will be lost. Most importantly, students should not be intimidated by software that's difficult to use. To avoid this, the software must tell students when to push certain keys so they can receive further directions or clarification. The program should not stop or appear to be doing nothing without clues about what to do next. Good software anticipates points at which students are likely to need help; students always should have options for getting the program running again or going back to the beginning. Of course, the program must interpret student responses accurately and give proper feedback, and any 'function keys' the program refers to must be available on the computer.

19. Teachers can employ the package easily.   Many of the same considerations apply here as for students. Teachers should not have to step in very often to help students run the program. At the same time, explanations of how to handle problems should be sufficiently detailed so teachers are able to help students when necessary.

20. The program appropriately uses relevant computer capabilities.
The computer software you buy should take full advantage of the unique
aspects of your microcomputer. The computer should be used so that
students are directly and actively involved, rather than simply passively
observing. The program should simulate activities that are too expensive,
difficult, or dangerous to demonstrate in reality. All software should be well
suited to computer use and not better handled by other instructional means.
Finally, information about students' performance should be able to be stored
for retrieval.

21. The program is reliable in normal use.   Consistency is the key
here. You shouldn't have to take any special precautions every time you run
a certain program, nor should you have trouble loading the software into the
computer.

Notations

22. Evaluator recommendation.   Having reviewed the previous 21
items, you're now ready to make a recommendation. You have three
options: recommend the program with little or no change, recommend the
program only if certain changes are made, or reject the program.

23. Describe the major strengths of the package.   Your ratings of the
first 21 items, as well as any notes you make, should be the basis for
elaborating on the program's strengths.

24. Describe the major weaknesses of the package.   Same goes for this
item. Here are some examples of evaluation notes. **Strengths**: "The
laboratory simulation is specific and could be used instead of a real
laboratory situation." "The students will be able to control many of the
variables that affect their instruction." "The user support materials are
thorough and comprehensive." **Weaknesses**: "Some equations are incorrectly
graphed on the monitor." "The student only watches the monitor; no active
participation in the courseware." "The computer is nothing more than an
electronic textbook. The program does not require the student to interact
with the computer."

25. Describe the potential use of the package in classroom settings.
After you evaluate the first 21 items and the strengths and weaknesses of the
program, describe how you think the software package should be used in the
classroom. You might think the program would be best used with
individuals or only with small groups. Or the package might be used to
introduce a topic or to reinforce previous instruction. Or maybe the best
application for a specific program is a 'contest' in which teams of students
devise the best way to solve a problem.

With all of the software on the market these days, you want to make sure you buy the right materials. Don't buy anything unless you've tried it or unless some of your best teachers approve it. Finally, make every effort to speak with school people in other systems who have used and are satisfied with any software you plan to buy.

B. Hardware

After you have made some tentative choices of courseware and discovered which microcomputer is the best choice for running the majority of the courseware you have located, you are ready to follow this sequence of steps in selecting a microcomputer:

1. Try out a micro and to get some rudimentary skills so that you can run courseware of the type that you might want to use in your classroom. This might be at your school or through a friend who has a micro.

2. Locate a supportive person to help you get familiar with the micro. Have them show you how to sign on, put on several software programs that interest you and run them, and, perhaps, help you write a simple addition program so you can begin to understand what a program is.

3. Purchase a paperback such as *Computers for Everybody* by Jerry Willis and Merle Miller, or find another that you like by scanning such books at a computer store or a bookstore.

4. Study the steps they suggest and list questions that come to mind as you read the book.

5. After you have read the introductory paperback, visit a school, a business or a computer store where they will not press you to make a quick decision, and start to learn about the differences between the various micros. Ask the questions from your list. Then ask the salesman to demonstrate a simple software program such as Bank Street Writer for word processing. Once you feel you can explain this to your principal, ask for a demonstration of Personal Filing System. These two programs will be very useful to your principal and the school secretary as "starter" programs and may help you gain their support in your effort to purchase a micro.

6. Become familiar with locations where you can continue to improve your computer literacy and get training in the use of instructional software. Ask for self-instructional materials which you can use to practice your computer skills when you get access to a micro.

7. Ask people who have experience with micros where you can get training. Continue a systematic search for courseware you could use in your classroom. Your best bet will be teachers in schools similar to yours. Ask the math and science coordinator in your county schools office if s/he knows of anyone with a list of computer-using teachers. Some states have organizations of computer-using teachers and they can give you teacher names, as can

district personnel in districts that have a number of computers. Visit these teachers and learn about the software they are using. Develop relationships where you can share things you have in return for instruction in selecting courseware from your "mentor" teacher(s).

8. As you circulate and learn more about micros you will note that each school and its classrooms are set up differently to utilize micros. Thus we find that each micro installation is a custom piece of work, unlike using films, for example, where the utilization is quite standard from room to room.

9. Search for courseware through other channels such as computer sales organizations and institutions offering microcomputer instruction. At the same time look for training opportunities and courses that you may wish to take. Be sure to distinguish between courses set up to teach introductory material to students who hope to be computer programmers and those emphasizing utilization of software. The latter courses are what you want now; they will probably be offered at colleges and universities. Programming courses are frequently taught at community colleges; they are good to keep in mind for a later time if you should decide to learn to program.

10. Investigate the hardware that is a) used in other schools by teachers using it in a manner similar to your style, and b) that has good courseware available of the type you have evaluated as useful. These are key factors in your choice of hardware since you need to be able to preview hardware before you purchase it. You also should ascertain that the courseware that runs on that hardware will be effective for you.

11. Identify major uses of the hardware. For example, do you need word processing capability on your first micro?

12. Specify minimum requirements (like **48 K** of memory to run your word processing program) as well as preferred features (like color rather than black and white) for instructional programs.

13. Identify secondary uses, such as making class lists, as well as desirable features such as a graphics capability.

14. Decide about how much you can spend, now and later. The cost can range from $300 to $4000 or thereabouts for a microcomputer, two **disk drives** and a **monitor**. For word processing, you may choose either a letter quality or a dot matrix printer. A letter quality printer can cost from $600 to $2500. For instructional use, a small dot matrix printer for about $400 to $600 will serve your needs adequately. The dot matrix printer will also allow you to use graphics to create overhead projections and other instructional materials. We use a software program titled Executive Briefing System published by Lotus for this purpose. In order to print the graphics on paper for copying, we use the program Print O Grapher by Southwestern Data Systems. A **grappler card** will also accomplish this task for you.

15. Survey the field by talking to knowledgable people and visiting technical assistance centers such as those at your county schools office where

you can see many different makes of micros. Community colleges are also good places to see a number of micros in action.

16. Survey sources for purchasing a micro, including a local or regional computer store, a mail order supplier, and a manufacturer. The mail order supplier may have the lowest price, since few manufacturers sell directly to the customer. The hardware may come with the highest price at the computer store. You may find a computer salesperson who sells by telephone from his or her home, as we have. Buying from her/him may save you 20-30% of your costs. This is wise as long as you have checked out your purchases in advance and know what you wish to buy and how to install and use it.

17. Buy or lease the computer. This decision will be influenced by the amount of cash available and the terms of leases for the equipment you wish to purchase. If you get a knowledgable person to help you, you may even decide to buy a used micro through the classified adds.

CHAPTER SEVEN
HELPFUL
TECHNICAL
INFORMATION

In this section we will give some additional background on computers and list a variety of services including Micro-Sift, CONDUIT, CUE, and SOFTSWAP. We also talk about the possible advantage of setting up a network of micros using the CORVUS system. There is a growing number of organizations that can provide teachers with information about the use of microcomputers, and the ones we have mentioned are representative of a larger group.

Not too many years ago, the calculator we take for granted today could have passed for a computer. Calculators work with numbers. They add, subtract, multiply and divide. Computers work not only with numbers, but with alphabetic data. A computer can be programmed to repeat a function over and over using new or updated data every time. It can examine a list of numbers and find a particular item; it can alphabetize a list of names and addresses. It can logically evaluate information following a "program" and can then act on its findings.

It can perform complex mathematical operations and soon will be able to "think" like a human being in a limited sense. This type of programming is called "using artificial intelligence." IBM is working on a program called Epistle, which will present an executive with a file of typical letters and memos. S/he will be asked to correct them to make them reflect her/his "style." Then the program will be able to write new letters and memos, given certain basic content for each paragraph, in the style of the executive. A program such as this could be used to write proposals for state and federal funding in schools, exhibiting the personal style of the author.

A computer is to the human mind what a power saw is to the hand, a machine capable of extending speed and effectiveness. It can free the user from repetition, such as grading tests and reporting the results, instantly printing out the scores so the teacher can see what problems students are having and take corrective action. In a matter of seconds it can report which students are in the bottom quartile in fractions and which in multiplication, so patterns can be seen and instruction targeted to specific groups of students.

If the teacher wishes, the computer can then be programmed to offer a review of fractions and multiplication skills utilizing a game format to increase motivation. It can do this for individuals and for groups to reduce monotony and keep students interested. It can also identify specific problems a student has missed by type (fractions) and provide additional work until adequate mastery, as judged by the teacher in advance, is achieved.

The history of the development of computers is evolutionary, not revolutionary. However, in 1977 a series of events began that led to their consequent increased use in schools. This increase can be attributed to the micro's low cost, their utility in doing so many kinds of tasks, and their reliability, which is much better than the large computers. They are available when you want them, unlike mainframe computers where one signs on and waits for a chance like planes wait to land at a busy airport. They are less likely to break down than the big machines as they are not so complex.

Several services that will be helpful for educators are:

Northwest Regional Educational Laboratory
300 SW Sixth Avenue
Portland, Oregon 97204

The Northwest Lab operates a Computer Technology Program which includes a clearinghouse to assist educators. The purpose of the clearinghouse has changed from physical dissemination of courseware to dissemination of information about courseware. This reflects the increasing amount of courseware available from commercial sources. Many teachers also get courseware from the "public domain," that is, they copy other programs where this is allowed. These may have been funded by federal funds or they may have come from some other source where no commercial fee is required.

The clearinghouse is also involved in the evaluation of courseware. Table 1 on the next page indicates a rank order of educators' needs in the use of microcomputers. A group of 51 educators were surveyed in order to guide

TABLE 1   Rank-ordered Need for Service to Educators

SERVICE	DEGREE OF NEED (%)		
	HIGH	MODERATE	LOW
Information on software quality	94.2	5.8	0.0
Information on software sources	83.6	12.7	3.6
Staff development	69.0	25.5	5.5
Planning assistance	65.3	30.6	4.1
Information on hardware quality	47.8	41.3	10.9
Courseware development	46.8	36.2	17.0
Application of technology to our needs	46.7	53.3	0.0
Information on hardware sources	34.1	47.7	18.2

lab staff in planning their services. This data might help the administrators in your district with their planning for the utilization of microcomputers.

Of particular value to teachers and administrators is the clearinghouse publication *MicroSift News* which you can obtain from the lab address above. Each issue is filled with useful information.

> Minnesota Educational Computing Consortium (MECC)
> 2520 Broadway Drive
> St. Paul, Minnesota 55113

MECC is another center of expertise that will help you. MECC has purchased more than 1000 Apples over the years and has a fine catalog of both training manuals and instructional programs for the Apple II/IIe. Recently, MECC has purchased 2000 Ataris and they are now distributing materials for this micro. They recommend using the Apple for delivering instruction and the Atari (or the equivalent) for literacy training and other tasks that do not require an expensive machine.

As you will learn when you subscribe to a computer magazine for educators, there are many state and regional organizations which focus on the needs of educators. In the Far West we have

> Computer Using Educators (CUE)
> 1776 Educational Park Drive
> San Jose, California 95133.

CUE has over 8000 members across the country and puts on four conferences annually. These are major events with dozens of workshops with 1200-1500 teachers attending. It also publishes a newsletter that is extremely useful. CUE, together with the San Mateo County (California) Office of Education, sponsors SOFTSWAP, an exchange program that allows teachers to trade micro programs they have written for others created by teachers in the same curriculum area. Since all the programs are in the public domain, they can also be purchased for $10 per program. They run on the Apple, TRS-80, PET, Atari and COMPUCOLOR micro-processors. Their catalog can be ordered from

SOFTSWAP
San Mateo County Office of Schools
333 Main Street
Redwood City, California 94603

As you consider your microcomputer purchases, you should know about the CORVUS constellation possibility. If you are ready to purchase two or more micros, you may benefit from tying them together in order to have

More memory for student records;
Sharing of courseware among micros;
Sharing of printer and graphics peripherals among micros; and
Control of student users.

Information about this equipment can be obtained from

CORVUS Systems
2029 O'Toole Avenue
San Jose, California 95131
Phone 408 946-7700

As you consider the exciting possibilities of utilizing microcomputers in your school, you may benefit from answering some questions of accountability developed by John J. Beck, Jr., in *The Directive Teacher:* (12)

1. Will the addition of computers aid in mastering the school curriculum?
2. Does a computer literate administration and faculty exist?

3. Is the district willing to budget funds to achieve computer literacy among its administrators and faculty if the need exists?
4. What are the relative characteristics of each system being considered?
5. What are the standard software package options of each system being considered?
6. What are the relative support services available for each system being considered?
7. Does any educationally sound courseware exist for the curriculum you need to deliver?(12)

The clear implication is that the district needs to set up a task force to study the curriculum before purchasing software and hardware. Each of us might ask these questions in a different manner and we encourage you to reword them to meet your local needs.

Great potential lies ahead for the increased use of microcomputers in schools. Many districts have begun to purchase them in large numbers; this will make it profitable for publishers to develop high quality courseware. Certainly we should insist that publishers of state adopted texts do this immediately so that teachers will have sound courseware to accompany these texts. As good courseware becomes available, it will carry educational activity into home, business and government settings. This is great news, for school people have often felt that education should be conducted in a variety of settings. Powerful education occurs when there is a coordinated effort between school, home and work place. The microcomputer may be a key mechanism for advancing this vision.

CHAPTER EIGHT
COMPUTER MAGAZINES AND RESOURCES

The following list of computer magazines and other print resources is representative of the rich variety of materials on the market for educators.

80 MICROCOMPUTING
P.O. Box 981
Farmingdale, New York 11737
603/ 924-3873
$18 per year

APPLE ORCHARD
P.O. Box 1493
Beaverton, Oregon 97075
$10 per year

APPLE SAUCE
20013 Pricetown Avenue
Carson, California 90746
213/637-8917

CLASSROOM COMPUTER LEARNING
P.O. Box 266
Cambridge, Massachusetts 02138
$12 per year

CLASSROOM COMPUTER NEWS: THE MAGAZINE FOR TEACHERS
AND PARENTS
Intentional Education
341 Mt. Auburn Street
Watertown, Massachusetts 02172
Published 8 times per year
$19.95 per year

CLOSING THE GAP (Special Education)
Dolores Hagen, Publisher
P.O. Box 68
Henderson, Minnesota 56044
Published 6 times per year
$15 per year

COMPUTER TOWN USA
P.O. Box E
Menlo Park, California 94025
$16 per year

THE COMPUTING TEACHER
Department of Computer and Information Science
University of Oregon
Eugene, Oregon 97403
$14.75 for 9 issues

COURSEWARE MAGAZINE
School of Business and Administrative Sciences
California State University
Fresno, California 93740
$15.95 for one year

Computer Magazines

CREATIVE COMPUTING
P.O. Box 789-M
Morristown, New Jersey 07960
800/631-8112
$12 for 12 issues

EDUCATIONAL COMPUTER
P.O. Box 535
Cupertino, California 95015
$12 for one year

ELECTRONIC EDUCATION
Suite 220
1311 Executive Center Drive
Tallahassee, Florida 32301
914/ 735-4970
$10 per year

ELECTRONIC LEARNING
Scholastic Inc.
730 Broadway
New York, New York 10003

HANDS ON
8 Eliot Street
Cambridge, Massachusetts 02138

INFO WORLD
375 Cochituate Road, Box 880
Framingham, Massachusetts, 01701
800/343-6474
$25 for one year

INTERFACE AGE
16704 Marquardt Avenue
Cerritos, California 90701
213/926-9540
$18 for one year

KILOBAUD MICROCOMPUTING
80 Pine Street
Petersborough, New Hampshire 03458
603/924-3873
$25 for one year

MEAN BRIEF
256 North Washington Street
Falls Church, Virginia 22046
703 536 2310

NIBBLE
P. O. Box 325
Lincoln, Massachusetts 01773
617/259-9710
$17.50 for 8 issues

ON COMPUTING
70 Main Street
Petersborough, New Hampshire 03458
800/258-5485

ON LINE
24695 Santa Cruz Highway
Los Gatos, California 95030
$7 for 36 issues

OUTPUT
666 Fifth Avenue
New York, New York 10103
$18 for one year

PERSONAL COMPUTING
1050 Commonwealth Avenue
Boston, Masssachusetts 02215
$14 per year

PERSONAL COMPUTING?
P.O. Box 13916
Philadelphia, Pennsylvania 19101
$18 per year

PROGRAM DESIGN, INC.
11 Idar Court
Greenwich, Connecticut 06830
203/661-8799

RECREATIONAL COMPUTING
1263 El Camino Real, Box E
Menlo Park, California 94025
$12 per year

SOFTSIDE
6 South Street
Milford, New Hampshire 03055
800/258-1790
$18 per year

SOFTTALK
10432 Burbank Blvd.
North Hollywood, California 91601
213/980-5074
Complimentary

TEACHING AND COMPUTERS
Scholastic Inc.
730 Broadway
New York, New York 10003
Published 8 times per year
$19 per year

TEACHING * LEARNING * COMPUTING
Seldin Publishing Inc.
1061 S. Melrose, Suite D
Placentia, California 92670
Published 10 times per year

In addition to these magazines we have found the following paperbacks helpful (we use an Apple II).

Apple II User's Guide
Lon Poole, et. al.
Osborne/McGraw Hill 1981
Berkeley, California

Computer Dictionary
Charles and Roger Sippl
Howard W. Sams and Co. 1980
Indianapolis, Indiana

Basic: A Self Teaching Guide 2nd Edition
Robert L. Albrecht, et. al.
John Wiley and Sons 1978
New York, New York

Practical Guide to Computers in Education
Peter Coburn, et. al.
Addison Wesley 1982
Reading, Massachusetts

The Book of Apple Computer Software: 1982 ·
James Sadlier and Jeffery Stanton
The Book Co.
Lawndale, California

The Computer in the School: Tutor, Tool, Tutee
Robert P. Taylor, Editor
Teacher's College Press
New York, New York

The Computer Age: A Twenty Year View
Michael L. Dertouzos and Joel Moses, Editors
MIT Press 1980
Cambridge, Massachusetts

Dozens of books relating to microcomputers are listed in the Creative Publications Catalogue, P.O. Box 10328, Palo Alto, California, 94303. Becoming familiar with software of interest, including courseware in your area, involves continual data gathering. Most people who use computers join "user clubs" to keep up to date on general software available. This book includes a listing of available software in a later section.

Learning about the many publications relating to your interest in micros has already been covered, with two important exceptions. First, you should know about the

Microcomputer Index
Microcomputer Information Services
2464 El Camino Real
Box 247
Santa Clara, California 95051

which offers bibliographic information on over 1200 articles and reviews each quarter. It costs $22 per year. Second, you may refer to the following list of software catalogs and directories.

CHAPTER NINE
MICROCOMPUTER SOFTWARE CATALOG AND DIRECTORY LIST

EDUCATION

1983 Classroom Computer News Directory of Educational Computing Resources
Intentional Educations
341 Mt. Auburn Street
Watertown, Massachusetts 02172
$14.95

Courseware Report Card
150 West Carob Street
Compton, California 90220
Two editions (elementary and secondary) appear five times annually
$49.95 per year

Education Software Directory
Apple II Edition
Sterling Swift Publishing Co.
P.O. Box 188
Manchaca, Texas 78652
$9.95

EPIE & Consumers Union
P.O. Box 620
Stony Brook, New York 11790
$75-300 depending on service

The International Council for Computers in Education (ICCE)
Department of Computer and Information Science
University of Oregon
Eugene, Oregon 97403

Large, nonprofit computer-educator organization; individual memberships
$16.50. Membership includes subscription to the *Computing Teacher*

Microcomputer Directory: Applications in Educational Settings
Write to Gutman Library
Appian Way
Cambridge, Massachusetts 02138
$15 A guide to computer projects nationwide

Microcomputer Software and Information for Teachers
Northwest Regional Education Laboratory
300 Southwest Sixth Avenue
Portland, Oregon 97204

Software reviews are published for an average cost of $4 to $5. To access
Resources in Computer Education, the needed data base, your school must be a
member of Bibliographic Retrieval Services(BRS), Inc. for a one time
membership fee of $150. Write to BRS, 1200 Route 7, Latham, New York,
12110.

Resource Handbook
Technical Education Research Centers
8 Eliot Street
Cambridge, Massachusetts 02168
$10 plus $2 for shipping

School MicroWare
Dresden Associates
P.O. Box 246
Dresden, Maine 04342
$20

Special Education Computer Technology Online Resource
SECTOR Project for Exceptional Children
UMC 68
Utah State University
Logan, Utah

Send self-addressed envelope for evaluation form or list of companies that offer
preview copies.

MARCK No 2
MARCK 280 Linden Avenue
Branford, Connecticut 06405
$4.95

Queue Catalog No. 4
Queue
5 Chapel Hill Drive
Fairfield, Connecticut 06432

Selected Microcomputer Software
Opportunities for Learning, Inc.
8950 Lurline Avenue
Chatsworth, California 91311
Free

Scholastic Microcomputer Instructional Materials
Scholastic Inc.
904 Sylvan Avenue
Englewood Cliffs, New Jersey 07632
Free (especially reliable)

K-12 Micromedia
P.O. Box 17
Valley Cottage, New York 10989
Free (especially reliable)

OTHER FIELDS

Radio Shack TRS-80
Applications Software Sourcebook
Radio Shack
Box 17400
Fort Worth, Texas 76102
$1

TRS-80 Software Source
COMPUTERMAT
P.O. Box 1664
Lake Havasu City, Arizona 86403
$6 per issue; $15 per year

80 Software Critique
RCW Microcomputing Services
P.O. Box 134
El Dorado, California 95623
$7 per issue; $24 per year

Atari Program Exchange
Atari Inc.
P.O. Box 427
155 Moffett Park Drive
Sunnyvale, California 94086

CHAPTER TEN
COURSEWARE FOR ELEMENTARY AND SECONDARY TEACHERS

A. Elementary

The computer has arrived and teachers are asking questions such as "How can a computer help me to become a better teacher?"; "What curriculum changes need to be made?"; and "How do I find software that is applicable to my situation?"

The computer can help the teacher in many ways. It can assist the teacher with time consuming administrative tasks such as test construction, test scoring, recording test scores, record-keeping, student files, achievement profiles and class schedules. With this administrative help from the computer, the teacher has more time to plan for the use of the computer in instruction. Instructional modes for using the computer include drill and practice, tutorial, games and simulations. A word processing program can be used to teach writing and editing.

When computers are installed in a school without a specific administrative or instructional purpose, they are often misused and become toys for running game after game. Consequently, teachers and administrators should be trained to use the computers prior to or in conjunction with their arrival at the school.

In terms of curriculum changes that need to be made in order to use the microcomputer one can follow this rule: "Make permanent changes in the curriculum once you have courseware that teaches the objectives best taught by the computer." To identify areas for computer-assisted instruction, the "computer committee," should meet with the curriculum committee and thoroughly review courses to locate objectives that could be taught more effectively with the computer. Then committee members initiate a search to find courseware that works well to teach the objectives. This "search for applicable software" usually involves contacting teachers in other districts to see what courseware they are using.

Courseware tells the computer what to do: what to display on the monitor; what responses should be given to the learner; what remarks to give for incorrect and correct replies and more. Designed to make educational objectives obtainable, courseware is available in a variety of curriculum areas. In this chapter we will discuss three instructional forms: Drill and Practice, Tutorial, and Simulations. We will describe five Utility programs and then close with some suggested courseware for teaching computer literacy. Courseware with one * is worth considering; two ** indicate the program is recommended.

Drill and Practice

This is the most commonly used courseware in education. Its purpose is to reinforce basic skills, a task the computer does extremely well. These programs provide the students with a number of basic questions generated either by the computer itself or by the teacher. Drill and practice programs have the ability to tally a student's correct and incorrect responses, and

Math Drill and Practice

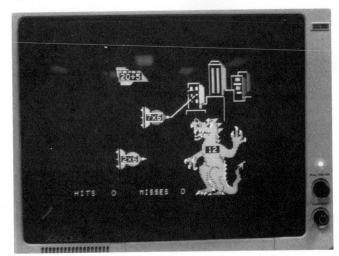

frequently will report to the teacher the number of correct and incorrect answers. They may also recommend and provide extra practice if this is appropriate. Students receive feedback from drill and practice programs. This can be as simple as yes, great, or O.K., or an elaborate pictoral response with a lot of movement on the screen. Descriptions of several drill and practice programs are seen below.

Mathematics

** *SRA Computer Drill and Instruction*
Science Research Associates
Grade Level
Level A   1 & 2
Level B   3 & 4
Level C   5 & 6

A comprehensive program for all elementary grade levels either for enrichment or remediation. Content of the program includes:

Whole Numbers	Division
Addition	Fractions
Subtraction	Decimals
Multiplication	

When a student is placed in the program, he is automatically given a placement test for an appropriate starting lesson. When the student shows an 80% or better on a lesson, he moves forward; a 51% to 79% has the student repeat the lesson. Instructional help is built into the program so that if a student presses a ?, the tutorial mode goes into effect. The managed version can print problems to be used as worksheets and provides reports to the teacher on individual or group progress.

** *Fact Track*
Science Research Associates
Grade Level- 1 to 6

A timed program for drill on addition, subtraction, multiplication and division skills. The program helps students develop quick responses to arithmetic facts. The computer reports the speed and the performance of the student and also shows those problems where there was difficulty. The program can be set at varying degrees of difficulty and speed.

** *Milliken Math*
Milliken Publishing Company
Grade Level- 1 to 6

A structured drill and practice program for basic math operations. Each sequence contains problems ranging from simple to complex, enabling the teacher to place the student at the appropriate level. Proficiency is set at 70% for mastery; a score of 30% moves the student to a lower level. Correct answers are reinforced by a WOW!, You Did It!, Great !, and so forth, while the incorrect answer elicits a second chance. If the student answers incorrectly twice, the computer will then flash the correct answer. The program provides a management system for teachers to assist in placement and tracking of students.

** *Estimation*
Minnesota Educational Computing Consortium
Volume 4
Grade Level- 3 to 6

Designed to test a student's ability to estimate an answer in the areas of addition, subtraction, multiplication and division. The program can be used either as a group game or for individual practice.

** *Math Game*
Minnesota Educational Computing Consortium
Volume 4
Grade Level- 2 to 6

Competition is set up as a random drill. Math Games provides students with opportunities to practice addition, subtraction, multiplication and division skills. The level of difficulty is determined by the age and ability of the student. Scores are totaled from the time taken and the number of tries. Bonuses are awarded according to the total time taken to answer the problems, player's age and grade level, as well as the percent of correct answers. At the end of the game the final score is displayed on the screen and the winner is acknowledged.

Reading

** *Comprehension Power*
Sections D, E and F
Milliken Publishing Company
Grade Level- 4 to 6

An inductive comprehension-building program, Comprehension Power consists of reading selections that are interesting and informative. Once the student has read the story, questions are asked which cover a total of twenty-five skills in five major areas:

Literal Understanding
Interpretation
Analysis
Evaluation
Appreciation

Comprehension Power also has a management section for teacher use in scheduling, placement, reading rate and checking student progress.

Tutorials

Tutorials are aimed at teaching concepts when the student has little or no prior knowledge of the subject matter involved. Guiding the learner from the lowest level, a good tutorial will lead the learner through the process for a better understanding of the material. Graphics or words may be used to explain or illustrate ideas. When it comes to the answers, tutorials will explain the reason why answers to the question or questions were incorrect if this is appropriate. When the student is progressing with proficiency, the tutorial will jump the student to a higher level. When the reverse is true, the student is re-routed back to the rules and a simpler series of questions.

Use of Graphics

Language

** *Word Structure*
Sections A, B, C and D
Micro Systems 80
Borg-Warner Corporation
Grade Level- 4 to 6

Designed to help students communicate effectively with emphasis on the structural changes in words, Word Structure covers the following concepts:

Capitalization/Abbreviation
Spelling/Syllables
Singular/Plurals
Possessives
Degrees of Comparison

The program contains a management system that tracks student progress and allows the teacher to see a student profile of work completed.

** *Prefixes*
Minnesota Educational Computing Consortium
Volume 5
Grade Level- 2 to 6

Offering instruction in the use of the prefixes *un-, re-, dis-, pre-,* and *in-,* this program provides students with activities to develop their recognition and comprehension skills. Following each activity a summary score of their progress is displayed on the screen. Students are asked to transfer their scores to a score sheet. Reinforcement is provided after each lesson from worksheets.

Simulations

Whether it be a trip to the moon, a trip on the Oregon Trail or the sale of lemondade at the corner stand, simulations will provide students a model of a real life or fantastic situation that they might never have the opportunity to encounter in the classroom (or in real life!)

Simulations allow students to use their imagination to explore and try something new to see what happens. To successfully use simulations, there are some questions to be considered.

1. How many variables are there in the program?
2. Is there one solution strategy that works every time, or many different ones?
3. Does the program include any random events?
4. What kinds of teacher support materials come with the program?

If it is at all possible, follow up on the simulation activity by asking your students questions about the activity. What information did they gain by trying different manuevers? What do they think would happen next? What worked best for them? What would happen if . . . ?

A good simulation will have logical thinking as a basic objective of the program. It will include clear directions and graphics. Some simulations will have math as an integral part of the program. The following computer simulations have proven to be well liked and appropriate for elementary students. This key may be helpful when selecting simulations.

D=Directions
L=Logical Thinking
M=Mathematics
G=Graphics

** *Lemonade*
Apple Computer Inc.
Level: Elementary

Lemonade is a mathematics and economics program in which students compete with others in a business simulation. While running the stand they are asked to make a number of decisions that relate to the amount of profit they will make. Includes keyed experiences D, L, M and G from the table above.

** *Wumpus*
Minnesota Educational Computing Consortium
Level: Elementary
Volume 3

Wumpus is a program in which the student searches a series of rooms in the shape of a duodecahedron looking for the fearsome Wumpus. (D and L)

** *Oregon Trail*
Minnesota Educational Computing Consortium
Level: Elementary
Volume 6

Oregon Trail is a mathematics and economics program in which students simulate a trip on the Oregon Trail from Independence, Missouri to Oregon City, Oregon. (D, M and L)

** *Hammurabi*
Apple Computer Inc.
Level: Elementary

Hammurabi is a mathematics and economics program in which students become ruler of Ancient Summerio. They must plan ahead to buy, sell, and plant grain along with feeding the growing population. (D, M and L)

** *Dungeon Campaign*
Synergistic Software
Level: Elementary

Dungeon Campaign is a simulated treasure hunt through a five-level maze. Students must avoid hazards as well as strange animals and beings. (D and L)

** *Civil War*
Minnesota Educational Computing Consortium
Level: Elementary
Volume 3

Civil War is a mathematics and economics program in which students pit themselves against decisions made in 14 original Civil War battles. By making correct decisions, students could change history (L, M and G)

* *Wilderness Campaign*
Synergistic Software
Level: Elementary

Wilderness Campaign simulates a journey through a treacherous wilderness with exciting hazards. The goal is to reach the castle. (D, G and L)

* *Mad Venture*
Micro Lab
Level: Elementary

Mad Venture is a simulation in which students use their imagination and cunning to find treasures, stay alive, and see the movie. (D and L)

** *Cranston Manor*
O'Sierra On Line Systems
Level: Elementary

Cranston Manor is a superb simulation/adventure game with outstanding graphics in which students search for sixteen treasures in a Victorian House. (L and G)

** *Mystery House*
O'Sierra On Line Systems
Level: Elementary

Mystery House is an excellent simulation/fantasy game in which students search out a treasure and solve mysteries inside a Victorian House. (D, L and G)

** *Odyssey Adventure*
Synergistic Software
Level: Elementary

Odyssey Adventure is a complex simulation written in Old English, where students explore an island in the Dreaded Saragaol Sea, looking for treasure and adventure. (D, L and G)

** *Zork I and Zork II*
Info Comm

Zork is a high level simulation in which students explore the great underground empire. It is a game of adventure, danger, and low cunning where they can explore the most amazing territory ever imagined by humans. The program must be answered in "complete sentences." (D and L)

** *Odell Lake*
Minnesota Educational Computing Consortium
Level: Elementary
Volume 4

Odell Lake simulates a food web in a Minnesota lake. The student takes the role of a fish and tries to survive. After role playing all the fish, the student is shown the relationships between the various animals. (D, G and L)

** *Odell Woods*
Minnesota Educational Computing Consortium
Level: Elementary
Volume 4

Odell Woods simulates a food web found in Northern Minnesota. The student takes the role of an animal and tries to survive. After role playing all the animals, the student is shown the relationships between the various forest inhabitants. (D and L)

** *Solar Distance*
Minnesota Educational Computer Consortium
Level: Elementary
Volume 4

This program teaches the concept of distances in space by having students take trips between planets in the solar system. The student chooses his mode of transportation and also learns his weight based on the gravity of other planets. (D, G, M and L)

Utility Programs

Utility programs are tools that teachers can use for such purposes as programming (Apple Pilot), graphics creation (EZ-Draw and Koala Pad), creation of puzzles (Crossword Magic) and grade management (Teacher's Aid). The following programs are worth your consideration * or recommended **.

* *Apple Pilot*
Apple Computer Company
Level: Adult

Pilot (available for most microcomputers used in schools) is an authoring system that allows a teacher with no programming knowledge to custom design computer assisted instruction for students. Most versions of Pilot allow the teacher to include graphics designs and sound effects. Some of the more advanced versions include a student response timer, use voice synthesizers, game paddles, graphics boards and light pens.

** EZ-Draw 3.3
Sirus Software
Level: Grade 7 to
Adult

EZ Draw is a professional tool for developing graphic images. The software includes twenty different fonts and can utilize all colors. Simple one-character commands allow the user to reverse, slant, rotate or mirror type faces and images in any part of the picture in any combination. They may also be expanded or compressed horizontally and vertically.

Koala Pad
Koala Technologies Corporation
Pre-School to Adult

The Koala Pad is a small graphics board that uses a stylus (or even your finger) to draw different shapes, sizes of lines and curves. A "pointing menu" allows the use of different colors to fill shapes, select backgrounds, "erase" lines, magnify images and save and load pictures. The use of a graphics program or graphics printer card allows the drawing to be printed.

** Crossword Magic
L & S Computer Ware
Adult

Crossword Magic is a teacher utility program that allows the computer to design a graphically pleasing crossword puzzle. The program accepts the desired words and automatically sizes and fits the words together. If a word does not fit, the program holds the word until there is a spot for the word. After the clues are entered, the computer automatically numbers the clues and prints the puzzle. Twenty puzzles may be stored on a disk.

* Teacher's Aid
Dr. Daley's Software
Adult

Teacher's Aid is a menu driven grade management program. The program features easy updating of grades, letter or point grades and a variety of grade averaging methods. Averaging methods include weighted scores, possible scores, tables and percentages. Student reports may be displayed on the screen or printed and can include grade totals, averages, missing assignments and assignment summaries.

Computer Literacy

Now that you are familiar with some courseware for teaching with computers, you need to be aware of ways to teach about computers. This type of instruction is typically titled Computer Literacy, and there appear to be as many ideas about what it is as there are notions of literacy in English. In our view, a simple approach to computer literacy for elementary students would include teaching skills related to 1) how the computer works; 2) what a computer can and cannot do; and 3) what the future holds in terms of computer use. Some school districts also offer students a chance to learn simple computer programming through "hands on" experiences with microcomputers. The following programs have worked well for us in computer literacy training.

** *Computer Discovery*
Science Research Associates
Grade Level- 4-Up

Based on making students computer literate so they may take advantage of computers in the years ahead, Computer Discovery covers the social impact and historical background of computers. It also deals with elementary computer programming. Students work directly with the computer and are guided by a workbook for follow-up and reinforcement. The entire program takes about six weeks, depending upon the ability and interest levels of the students.

** *The Computer Is Here- A Computer Time Activity Box*
Educational Insights
Grade Level- Upper Elementary
and Junior High

An activity box that can serve as a supplement to instruction in computer literacy. Upon completion, a student will have worked through a pre-programming course. The cards cover various activities including computer applications, computer components, hardware and software, loading and running a computer and much more. The final steps include the typing and execution of a computer program. Activities may be performed with or without a computer.

Computer programming often requires thinking skills and technical training that are well beyond the level of computer literacy. Elementary students can learn to design and develop computer programs. A few materials have been developed to help them do so. Perhaps the best known of these is the **LOGO** program developed at the Massachusetts Institute of Technology by Seymour Papert.

** *Creative Programming for Young Minds*
Creative Programming Inc.
Grade Level- 3-Up

The program consists of various levels of workbooks that were created to enrich the minds of young children. In conjunction with reading the workbook, the student interacts with the computer as he/she progresses through the lessons. Upon completion of a book a student has the opportunity to complete a few independent projects. When these are completed, a copy of the project can be sent to the company and, in turn, the student will receive a special programmer's card. Special books are also available to provide students with experiences in graphics.

Acceptance of microcomputers in the elementary schools will depend on the quality of courseware that is available to teachers. Many of the qualities that are considered in textbook selection will be significant in courseware choices. We suggest that you study the evaluation forms for courseware seen in the chapter Courseware Evaluation.

B. Secondary

Courseware for junior and senior high school students is gradually improving in quality and more choices are becoming available. Many of the courseware programs described below have been reviewed by author Roger Walden at the Microcomputer Resource Center at the Office of the Superintendent of the Los Angeles County Schools. We mention this to suggest that you locate a similar facility in your area where you can preview courseware before making a purchase recommendation to your district. If your county office has not yet arranged to gather courseware from vendors, by all means encourage them to do so.

** *Volcanoes*
Earthware Computer Services
P.O. Box 30039
Eugene, Oregon 97403
System requirements:
Apple II/IIe Applesoft, 48k
Game-Simulation
Grade Level: 8 and up;
Physical Science

Volcanoes is a simulation geared towards the area of the earth sciences. This game helps in teaching the value of cooperation in conducting scientific investigations and applying the scientific method to volcanology and geology.

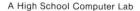

A High School Computer Lab

This simulation game is played by two to four players in the mythical land of Wrangelia. This mythical land is very similar to the northwest coast of North America. Each player assumes the role of a volcanologist who is assigned to study and predict volcanic eruptions. The object of the game is to predict when an eruption will occur. To meet this objective each player has to use his limited funds to choose among the seven types of scientific investigations. These investigations and the cost for each is displayed on a menu.

At the end of each turn the player must interpret the results of his investigation and decide if any volcanoes are going to erupt. Since there is not enough money in his budget to investigate all the volcanoes, he must make a number of calculated guesses.

At the beginning of each turn, each player is assigned a new skill level and more research money is based on his performance from the previous round. The better your performance, the easier it is to get more funding.

After the first round, eruptions occur often and surprises begin to occur. One of these surprises is a trip to a gambling casino where the player can win more money. This really makes the game exciting and very unpredictable.

Some knowledge of earth science is needed to give the game meaning. Once a player begins to understand the terminology and the results of the various investigations, the game is much easier to understand.

The graphics in this game are of the highest quality and enhance the program.

We liked this program; it is excellent.

* *Vocabulary Baseball*
J&S Software
140 Reid Avenue
Port Washington, New York 10050
System Requirements:
Apple II, Applesoft, 32k
Drill and Practice-Game
Grade Level: 8 and up
Language Arts

Vocabulary baseball is a multiple-choice vocabulary drill game geared towards the area of language arts.

To play this game the player needs to know the basics of baseball and have a good vocabulary. The object of the game is to get the highest score possible. To start the game a player selects the level of difficulty, a single being the easiest, a triple being the hardest. Once he has chosen the level of difficulty, the player is presented with a word and a choice of four definitions. If he responds with the correct choice, he scores a hit and goes to the base chosen by the difficulty. If he chooses the incorrect response then it is an out. The game lasts one, two or three innings. Each inning has three outs.

We found the graphics to be entertaining at first, but later on it slowed the game down considerably.

There were a number of errors in spelling and definitions. A game of this type should not have any errors.

The words used were appropriate for high school aged students. We felt this game had some educationl value.

** *Vocabulary Skills: Prefixes, Suffixes and Root Words*
Milton Bradley Company
43 Shaker Road
East Longmeadow, Massachusetts 01028
System Requirements:
Apple II/IIe, Applesoft, 48k
Tutorial
Grade level: 6-9
Language Arts

This program is designed to supplement instruction in the language arts. The object of this program is to master prefixes, suffixes and root words. Each lesson has its own instructions and examples. The student is given the option of review, taking a five item practice quiz or mastery quiz.

There are three phases of the tutorial: instructions, practice or mastery. The material is presented in a multiple-choice, matching or true-false format. If the student responds incorrectly, the program tells him to TRY AGAIN.

The lessons build from one to another, so what is learned in the first lesson is carried over to the next lesson and built upon sequentially.

The program presents material in a wide variety of ways, thus avoiding boredom. It possesses the most important qualities of a good tutorial: thoroughness, clarity, plenty of examples, reinforcement and practice. The program has a reward for doing a good job called "Alien Raiders." There is also a little guy called Ol' Coach Syllable, who gives great pep talks along the way.

We found the program easy to use and appropriate for this grade level. We really liked it.

** *Lessons in Algebra*
George Earl
1302 South General McMullen
San Antonio, Texas 78237
System Requirements:
Apple II/IIe, Applesoft, 48k
Tutorial-Drill & Practice
Grade Level: 9-12
Mathematics

Lessons in Algebra is a tutorial–drill and practice program. The program consists of nine learning units. Each unit provides examples and theories. As the student completes each lesson a series of true/false or multiple-choice questions check for understanding. If the student gives the correct response he continues the lesson. If he gives an incorrect response, the program will back up to the appropriate level for further instructions. When the lesson is completed, a cumulative percentage score is given.

This is a very simple program to use. The input is minimal, instructions are clear and an incorrect response prompts immediate reinforcement. The large print makes the program easy to read.

We found this to be a very good program for high school math students.

CHAPTER ELEVEN
USING LOGO

Welcome to Logo! These words introduce the learner to the wonderful microworld of Logo. Logo is derived from the Greek word logos, which means thought or word. It is a unique combination of programming language, learning theory and educational philosophy. It has rapidly become the foundation for computer instruction in many school districts.

BACKGROUND

Logo was developed by Seymour Papert with help from Wallace Feurzeig and Daniel Bobrow in the late 1960's. It was further refined in the Artificial Intelligence Laboratory at the Massachusetts Institute of Technology.(13).

The original research on Logo was closely related to mathematics. The designers wanted to create a problem solving language that was applicable to a wide range of topics. They felt that programming on a computer could illustrate hard-to-teach math concepts and provide a laboratory-like environment where one could experiment with abstract ideas. This plan evolved into an effort to work more broadly with discovery learning patterned on a Piagetian approach. The designers believed that students learn best by doing, in this case programming the computer so that the student is in charge rather than just a respondent. Students are given control over powerful computational resources and in the process they may begin to understand concepts from math, science and problem solving.

Logo in the Classroom

The three basic components of Logo are turtle graphics, arithmetic and list processing (the manipulation of words and lists). The use of turtle graphics has been so popular that many people mistakenly believe that this represents Logo in its entirety.

There are many different forms of Logo on the marketplace today. Full scale Logo programs are available for the Apple II/IIe, Texas Instruments 99/4A, Commodore 64 and the Atari 800. There are also modified programs that emphasize turtle graphics for the Apple II/IIe, TRS 80 Color Computer, Atari 400/800, IBM Personal Computer, PET, VIC 20 and the Commodore 64.

At the heart of Logo's success is its lack of complexity. Using simple commands, the learner positions the turtle and then moves it. A student begins by typing the name of the program preceded by the naming command TO. The student then simply moves the turtle (in turtle steps of course!) by giving it a command such as FORWARD 25. If the student wants to change the direction that the turtle will move, (s)he tells the turtle which direction to turn, and how many degrees to turn. For example, the command RIGHT 90 would turn the turtle to the right 90 degrees and it would be ready for another movement command. A simple turtle program looks like this.

```
TO SQUARE
FORWARD 50
RIGHT 90
FORWARD 50
RIGHT 90
FORWARD 50
RIGHT 90
FORWARD 50
END
```

For convenience, the student could also use the abbreviations of FD (FORWARD) and RT (RIGHT). Through trial and error the student soon learns how to move the Logo turtle (a triangle) where he wants it to go.

These simple commands and the learner's grasp of turtle movement make Logo a good choice as a vehicle for learning programming skills.

There are other benefits to consider as well. Logo is a procedural language. This means that it builds programs by combining commands. What is unique about Logo is that it can then take these programs and use them as steps in other procedures. Then the new programs can be used as steps in other procedures. One can quickly see the varying degrees of complexity that this can lead to. The programmer learns logical thinking steps in problem solving while organizing the procedures in the program on which (s)he is working.

Logo is also an **interactive** language. From the moment one learns the first simple steps, (s)he is working at the keyboard reacting to interesting program responses and, thus, learning. The student edits, revises and adds to what has been accomplished. In this way (s)he builds on previously learned concepts.

Logo Research

Logo has been studied in many different educational settings. Due to Logo's radical departure from most school mathematics curriculua, however, there has been little common ground on which to establish tangible objective changes. One example of this has been the Brookline Logo Project carried out in Brookline, Massachusetts.(14) Hard data was never obtained in this study because of the problems of devising and administering objective tests in the areas of problem solving and procedural thinking. The staff, however, reported some amazing success stories, ranging from students classified as academically gifted to those with learning disabilities. Logo also seemed to fit students with a variety of learning styles.

One of the most exciting Logo experiments is being carried out by Sylvia Weir of the Massachusetts Institute of Technology at the Cotting School for the Physically Handicapped in Boston.(15) Ms. Weir has been using Logo to help students with cerebral palsy effectively interact with a computer and improve their communication skills.

Pre-Logo Activities

Logo has been used successfully with all age groups. If you want to lead into Logo through other activities, however, you have several options.

There are many programmable devices that you can buy that will follow a path which you program. The most popular and reasonably priced example is Big Trac by Milton Bradley.

There is also a modified Logo program that has been developed by the Young People's Logo Association (YPLA) for younger children. Instead of the traditional Logo triangle this program uses a realistic turtle shape. The child makes the turtle go backward, forward, left and right through simple, one key commands.

Spinnaker's Delta Drawing also offers the learner a chance to manipulate computer graphics. This program is easier to use than Logo but lacks many of Logo's powerful capabilities. As an introduction to programming computer graphics, however, this program works well.

There are many Logo activities that can be practiced away from the computer as well. Younger students can learn the basis for turtle programming by becoming the turtle themselves. They can then follow simple programming commands such as "turn left" or "walk five steps". More experienced Logo users can write procedures out on paper and try to have others guess what the procedure will look like. There are, of course, variations in these two activities.

Clubs and Books

There are places the Logo teacher or student can turn for information or ideas. One of the best is the previously mentioned YPLA. This valuable support group provides a sharing of ideas and assistance to members. To join, send $25 (adult) or $9 (under 18) to YPLA, 1208 Hillside Drive, Richardson, Texas, 75081.

Another excellent resource for Logo teachers is Harold Abelson's book *Apple Logo,* published by BYTE/McGraw Hill. Abelson's book is really a user's guide that leads to many exciting Logo projects using graphics and language.

The International Council for Computers in Education (ICCE) has also published a new book of twenty three Logo lessons entitled *Logo in the Classroom.* These lessons are designed for elementary children. The price of the booklet is $11 and it can be obtained by writing to ICCE, 1787 Agate Street, University of Oregon, Eugene, Oregon, 97403.

Because of Logo's unique interaction capability with its users, it is difficult to describe it well in written format. The magic of Logo takes place in the learner's mind as (s)he quickly delves into a world of problem solving, editing and creation. Logo's designer, Seymour Papert says Logo has no threshold, no ceiling.(16) If this is true then we have merely scratched the surface of Logo's potential thus far.

In the Fullerton School District in Fullerton, California 1000 students are being introduced to LOGO by Media Specialist Mary Lou Olsen. Ms. Olsen sees the primary benefits of LOGO as a means for teaching 1) problem solving, and 2) higher level thinking skills. She previously taught critical thinking skills using puzzles played through computer software.

Some of the problems she encountered were the relatively high cost of the LOGO software ($200); the slow loading characteristics; the need to erase material as one works though the program; and the need for a thorough introduction since the material is quite different from other computer software her students have used. She reports very minor technical problems in using the program.

Ms. Olsen was successful in presenting LOGO to students and parents using the Manual chapter by chapter. She now uses the parents she trained in her first year as computer assistants in teaching the 1000 students she works with how to use the program. She faces the students in class-size groups and they sit on a carpet in the center of her computer laboratory. They see the material she is bringing up on the computer behind her on a large color monitor. After group instruction they return to the computers in pairs to try out the lesson of the day. Her laboratory is located in the District Media Center and as schools obtain the needed color monitor and computers she will make her presentations in school media centers.

CHAPTER TWELVE
USING COMPUTERS
IN THE
COMMUNITY COLLEGE

The information in this chapter will interest many readers who work in community colleges as well as teachers and administrators in elementary and secondary schools. The community colleges have much more experience in using computers than is true for public schools and they hence can give other readers ideas about computer courses and services now offered in community colleges which may be offered in elementary (services) and secondary (courses and services) schools in the future.

The use of computers in community colleges is quite different from operations in the elementary and secondary schools. The primary computer activity in the community colleges is instruction in programming and the various programming languages. Many of the students taking courses are planning careers in programming and related activities such as computer graphics. At the same time there are the service operations that are needed in any educational organization such as computer use in administration and instruction in the standard departments. We turn now to a description of the use of computers at two community colleges.

COOPERATIVE COLLEGE

At Cooperative College both mainframe and microcomputers are utilized extensively. The mainframe is a Honeywell DPS 8 which is used for business functions including budget, payroll and financial planning and for administrative tasks such as keeping student records, staff and faculty records, preparation of the catalog, scheduling and the preparation of transcripts.

There are several types of computers used for instruction, primarily microcomputers. In the mathematics and science courses the Apple II/IIe is dominant, whereas the business courses use several micros that offer CP/M capability in their standard configurations.

The history of computer use at the College is quite typical of community colleges. In the early years the College belonged to a consortium that included four area school districts. Gradually all the institutions increased their computer use and the College split off and acquired its own computers. In those days academic and administrative functions were separate, much as they are in high schools today. With increased computer use, a full time Computer Center Director was hired and academic and administrative functions were combined. This system has worked well, especially since the Computer Center staff have worked to support clients of the Center as well as key staff in other parts of the College. The Center has had adequate financial support and a good measure of autonomy.

The choice of equipment is critical and Cooperative chose well. They selected the Honeywell on-line system and have been pleased with its capability. It has taken less time to create appropriate software and to maintain the system than would have been true with another system they considered.

The most widely used software for the microcomputers is the word processing program WordStar. The next most popular program is SuperCalc, which is used in financial planning and instructor assignment. The micro is used for computer assisted instruction in courses and drill and practice where this is seen as appropriate. There is a strong effort made to use the computer only for those tasks that can be best accomplished by computer. Although the main course use of the micro is to teach programming, as it seems to be in most community colleges, there is an increased emphasis on interfacing various types of information with the computer. Practically every business and professional group has begun to use the computer and these new applications are an important influence in the field.

As we consider instruction, there are many tasks performed on the computer that could easily utilize other instructional approaches. The faculty at Cooperative, however, feel the most important use of the computer in instruction is in modeling and demonstrating ideas previously discussed on a theoretical basis. Examples would be molecular bonding or basic properties of physics.

There has been a concerted attempt to involve faculty in the use of computers. An Instructional Computer Committee was formed and representatives from each department were included. The Committee investigated software, hardware and implementation programs. Each member of the Committee was given a microcomputer and asked to encourage other faculty from their department to use it. In this manner a cadre of computer-oriented faculty has been developed.

The data processing department has seen a change in its enrollment patterns in the last several years which may be reflected in other community colleges as well. There has been a decline in enrollment in advanced courses and a large increase in first and second level courses. Administrators at Cooperative think that many of their advanced students are now taking courses in four year institutions as these programs develop. Thus the basic mission of the community college is being accomplished. Students are beginning their studies in the two year institution and moving on for completion in the four year institution.

Cooperative offers an interesting array of computer courses which give us yet another perspective on the two year college. These include:

Introduction to Data Processing
Introduction to Computers and Programming
Personal Computing- Software
Report Program Generator Programming
Beginning COBOL Programming
FORTRAN IV (arithmetic problem solving language)
Computer Operations (emphasizes hardware)
Introduction to BASIC
Data Processing Project (advanced work)
Advanced Report Program Generator
COBOL Tables (Table Handling)
COBOL Subprograms (linking subprograms)
COBOL Report Writer
Systems Analysis and Design
COBOL Keyed and Indexed Files
Data Processing Design

Word Processing is also taught in the Secretarial major. The emphasis on programming is certainly evident in this list. We turn now to view a second community college.

TECHNOLOGY COLLEGE

Technology College has a Computer Laboratory which occupies the second floor of the humanities building. The Lab has many types of equipment including four classroom microcomputer labs, three lecture rooms and a fifth classroom lab under development.

The main Lab has more than 50 terminals to a multi-language mainframe ITEL AS7 IBM which is housed at a sister institution, More Tech College. Technology College receives signals from More Tech by using the microwave antennae for a public broadcasting television station. Technology then uses hardwire to transmit to terminals throughout the campus. Various departments have their own terminals.

The main Lab is equipped with 15 Tektronix terminals which are capable of using CRT video display graphics. It also has 25 LA-120 printing terminals, 8 Viewpoint terminals, 6 Datamedica terminals and 6 microfiche transparency displays. The Lab can reproduce anything that utilizes the Tektronics terminals with hard copy computer print-out and there are plotters which will reproduce copy with ink on paper.

The four microcomputer labs each have 30 Apples and two or three printers. One lab also has 8 **modems** which are used to teach students how to use the modem. The fifth lab, which will open soon, will also have 30 micros as well as special equipment such as **Koala Pads, paddles, joysticks,** a **digitizer** board and color ink plotters. This lab is being especially equipped for use by Engineering and Drafting students and other students will use it as well.

The three lecture rooms each have multiple monitors for displays from the Apples or the mainframe in any language. They are also equipped with overhead projectors and videocassettes. All the labs and lecture rooms are used for regular instruction by the various departments as well as independent assignments.

Students may use the labs several hours each day, some evenings and for a few hours on Saturdays. Students are limited to one hour on the computer if other students are waiting; otherwise there is no time limit. Students provide their own word processing software when they are writing papers outside a word processing class. Tutors who are majoring in computer science are provided through the College Tutoring Center to assist students with programming problems. Other support is available through Proctors in the labs who help students sign on the various computer assisted instruction programs.

The Computer Lab provides a variety of services for faculty. They can obtain lists of their students with course grades that only show the student ID numbers and these can then be posted on classroom doors. The Lab will run a Scantron on sets of examinations which makes it possible for the instructor to have printouts indicating the mean, median and a histogram for each class. Faculty may also obtain item analyses indicating the number of students who selected each test item. These results may then be used to diagnose areas of weakness and guide faculty in preparing instruction to meet student needs.

Faculty may also arrange to use modems for research projects as long as funding is provided by their department or an outside source. The Lab also provides on-line testing for several departments including Political Science and Biology. Other Lab services include grade reporting, statistical analysis of grades and other data, inventories and class scheduling.

The Lab provides a 50 page Index of Computer Assisted Instruction Programs which are available and widely used by students. The Index is in the format of a library reference card. CAI programs cover the following areas of interest:

Accounting	Management
Music	Music
Astronomy	Nursing
Biology	Philosophy
Calculus	Physics
Chemistry	Police Science
Computer Science	Political Science
Economics	Psychology
Electronics	Real Estate
English	Secretarial Science
Finite Math	Spanish
Genetics	Special Education
Geography	Statistics
History	Technical Math
Italian	Trigonometry

Students are assigned to CAI programs as part of their coursework. They are given instructions for signing on to the system in the course syllabus; typically, they require little assistance once they are in the Lab.

Within the Computer Science and Business Departments the following courses are offered:

Word Processing on the Microcomputer
Survey of Business Data Processing
Introduction to FORTRAN APL
Principles of Computer Programming- APL
Principles of Computer Programming- FORTRAN
Computer Programming- BASIC
Computer Programming- COBOL
Computer Programming for Business- BASIC
Advanced BASIC for Business
Business Data Communications for the Personal Computer
Computer Literacy

It is interesting to speculate about the future role of the community colleges in computer education. It would appear that they will continue to play a major role in preparing students who will make a career in programming and other technical work related to the use of computers.

CHAPTER THIRTEEN
COMPUTERS FOR THE HANDICAPPED

The advent of high technology and the computer revolution have contributed to the development of methods to afford severely handicapped students the opportunity to communicate, to make dramatic gains in conceptual intelligence, receptive and expressive language, reading recognition and social-emotional skills.

Motor impairment in the severely physically handicapped child can hinder the ability to communicate, making these children totally dependent upon their audience to interpret their message. This is due to their inability to use their hands or arms to write or sign. Some physically handicapped children who cannot rely on oral communication find themselves in a uniquely powerless situation. These children may have complete intellectual capabilities but are restricted due to their neurological impairment.

In this chapter we will look closely at technological advances for the computer which can have significant impact on the severely handicapped child's ability to learn and communicate in everyday activities.

A. Computer Hardware for the Handicapped

The rapid development of hardware for handicapped persons to use in gaining access to microcomputers is one of the happiest stories in education

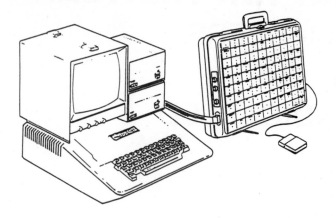

today. For any student, the micro can open new doors to learning and growth. For some of these handicapped students, the computer will offer the first real communication and intellectual opportunity they have ever experienced. It is our great pleasure to contribute to this possibility.

We turn now to some of the hardware that has worked in our situation.

Zygo 100 Communicator

The Zygo 100 is a communicator which consists of a rectangular box with 100 squares on the front panel. A drawing of the Zygo appears at the beginning of this chapter. Each square has a light which can be activated by a special switch on a cord attached to the box. The special switch is selected according to the needs of the student. The part of the body which offers the best control is utilized to activate the switch, whether it be the head, hand or foot.

The squares on the front panel can be filled with pictures, words, or other symbols, depending on what is to be communicated. Usually a student has a variety of face sheets for the panel so he can communicate basic needs, indicate answers to math problems and carry out other academic activities. The lights scan in rows across the panel. The student stops the scan at the appropriate row level and then on the square that he wishes to use to communicate. The rate of scan and selection of items is adjustable. There is a memory unit of fifteen items, so the individual can make sentences by selecting a number of items and then use a memory recall function to produce the items in the order selected. There is an alarm button which the student can use for calling for attention or help.

The device also has a special **interface** which connects the Zygo 100 to the Apple II/IIe computer. The front panel of the Zygo 100 has a special overlay with the letters and control keys that are found on the Apple II/IIe keyboard. The scanning mechanism and the special switch are then utilized to make entries into the computer. This allows the student who cannot physically use the keyboard access to the computer. It is generally a slow process and requires considerable patience and practice for success. It is worth it!

Express I

The Express 1 is a portable computer that enables the user to program words, phrases or sentences at 114 locations on the matrix display for a fast, efficient means of communication. Totally portable, it has overlays that are divided into rectangles. These rectangles are filled with letters, words or pictures, or whatever is necessary to meet the individual needs of students.

A light scans either by rows or columns. The student, by means of pointing, head control or movement of various parts of the body, will stop the light at the appropriate square he wishes to use to communicate. The rate of scan is adjustable. If a child is at the picture or symbol level when his/her selection is made, the corresponding word is then printed out on a **strip printer**.

Program levels for the Express I are:

Level 1 is predetermined;
Levels 2 and 3 are user programmable for up to 8 characters at each location; and
Level 4 is user programmable for up to 16 characters at each location.
The Express 1 can also serve as a text generator and as a data entry terminal with the Apple Computer Connector.

Express 2

Much like the Express 1, the Express 2 allows the students to enter information into the computer by means of a full *ASC II character set*. It can be programmed by the user to store words, numbers, computer instructions and relieve the user from the burden of entering information one character at a time.

The Express 2 can be connected to a computer either by a keyboard connector or an interface card. The keyboard interface mounts inside the computer and connects between the keyboard and the main logic board. A cable from the computer plugs into the serial output of the appropriate communication device. This permits the use of standard software programs and the standard keyboard operation is not affected.

Echo II Speech Synthesizer

The Echo II Speech Synthesizer consists of a plug in a speech board and amplifier for the Apple II/IIe computer. The heart of the Echo II is Texas Instruments' 5200 speech processor. More advanced than the circuit is Texas Instruments' Speak & Spell, which models the human vocal tract using Linear Predictive Coding; the Echo II stores only those parameters needed to describe each speech sound. This device along with the Echo II software allows the computer to speak. Although there are some limitations, it may also be used to make some commercial programs speak even though they were not explicitly designed to run with a speech synthesizer.

Switches

A wide variety of switches are commercially available. These can be adapted by an engineer if they do not meet specific needs. Also, customized switches can often be made to fit special needs. Selection of an appropriate switch involves considerations of positioning of the individual as he uses the switch, when at rest, and abnormal reflex activity. The most consistent, reliable and efficient motor response is the one which is selected for switch activation. **Game paddles** designed specifically for computer use may also be utilized.

Keyboard

Unicorn Keyboards by Unicorn Engineering Company of Oakland, California, can be connected to the Apple II/IIe. The keyboard is oversized (11.25 inches by 21.25 inches), light in weight and can easily be mounted on a wheelchair table for student use. The keys can be easily read and quickly activated.

The keyboard itself consists of 128 keys, and not all of them may be necessary in a given situation. Overlays are available and others can be developed, each with corresponding software to make it operational. A simple program is necessary to define the function of the keys and to instruct the interface card to scan.

B. Computer Programs for Use With People With Severe Physical Disabilities

Motor Training Games
Alternative Communication System Project
Child Development and Mental Retardation Center
University of Washington
Seattle, Washington

The disk includes 13 motor training games designed to allow nonstressful practice using 1 or 2 switches to refine motor abilities. The following is a list of programs from Motor Training Games found to be quite useful.

** *Davy's Digits*
Grade Level: Pre-school on
Input Methods: 1 or 2 switches

By use of a switch, children count out numbers. Time may be set to allow time for response. Two modes are available.

1. Simple Counting—The student presses the switch and the computer counts the number and displays it on monitors.

2. Matching—The student tries to match a random number by counting out that number with the switch. The upper limit is set by the teacher at a level between 1 and 9.

Davy's Digits provides a means not only for counting tasks but also allows the teacher to assess the student's ability to hit the switch the correct number of times.

** *Frog and Fly*
Grade Level: Pre-school on
Input Methods: 1 or 2 switches

When the program begins, a frog is sitting in the corner of the screen. While the fly is on the screen the switch is hit for the frog to catch the fly. Each time the fly will move faster across the screen. This program is used to increase motor control and ability to visually scan items on a screen from left to right.

** *Anti-Aircraft*
Grade Level: Pre-school on
Input Methods: 1 or 2 switches

Much like Frog and Fly, Anti-Aircraft displays a ship at the bottom of the screen. An airplane moves across the screen to be shot down by the ship. Once the switch is hit and the plane is shot down, the plane will explode and a man will parachute out.

The speed of the plane and its rate of acceleration can be set by the teacher. If the student misses, the speed of the plane will automatically drop.

** *Free-Throw Basketball*
Grade Level: Pre-school on
Input Methods: 1 or 2 switches

A basketball player is holding a ball ready to take a shot at the basket. Two modes are available:

1. One-switch demonstration for low functioning children, a non-fail situation, or it can be used to introduce the game.

2. Two-switch game where the speed and angle of the ball are selected prior to the shot. If the student misses, he can begin to modify the angle and the speed throughout by trial and error.

** *ABC Dragon*
Grade Level: Pre-school on
Input Methods: 1 or 2 switches

A letter will appear in a box on which a dragon is sitting. On the right side of the screen four letters and a red arrow will appear. The red arrow scans the four letters. The student must push the switch when the red arrow matches the letter that is in the box. If the letter matches, the dragon will "eat" the letter. If the ·switch is pressed when the letters do not match, a soft sound may be heard. All letters of the alphabet may be used in random order. The teacher may set the rate of scan, range of letters to be used and whether upper or lower case letters should be used. This program will assist in training students to scan and also develop their ability to match letters.

** *Word Burner*
Grade Level: Pre-school on
Input Methods: 1 or 2 switches

Uses the same format as ABC Dragon but uses words instead. Two modes are available: (1) Visual matching; and (2) Secret matching—word is not displayed under the dragon but is pronounced by the teacher making this an audio/visual task. A musical tune is played when the student responds correctly. Data on student performance can be printed out at the end of the lesson.

** *Academics With Scanning: Language Arts*
Grade Level: Grades 3 - 7
Input Methods: 1 or 2 switches

Switches are used to assist students in completing a simulated paper and pencil language arts activity on the computer. Programs on this disk are Word Attack, Crossword and Phonics Machine. The teacher has the ability to add word lists so students may work at their own level.

** *Academics With Scanning: Math*
Grade Level: Grades 3 - 7
Input Methods: 1 or 2 switches

This program makes use of the computer for "paper and pencil" math problems. The teacher can type in problems to be completed by students with the assistance of switches. Programs on this disk include: Addition with Carrying, Substraction with Borrowing, Multiple Digit Multiplication, Long Division, Constructive Geometry, Fractions and Story Problems.

Visual Matching; Note Joystick

** *Counting Bee*
S.V.E. Microcomputer Software
Edu-Ware Division
Grade Level: K - 3
Input System: Space Bar, Return and Escape

The target audience for Counting Bee is students with learning disabilities. For input, most entries require the use of just three keys. These are the space bar, return and escape. When numeric entries are necessary, non-numeric inputs are rejected.

Counting Bee is a **high resolution** animation that introduces children with little or no computer experience to basic numeric and quantitative concepts. Special features make this program worth adding to your courseware library:

* The system may be customized to meet the specific learning needs of individual children.

* It is entertaining and holds student's attention.

* In order to reinforce correct responses, sound effects and child-oriented melodies have been utilized.

* It contains a reporting system pertaining to the student's performance. This file allows the student to continue at a later time beginning where s/he left off.

* Student correction occurs at once.

Counting Bee has a total of eight modules that allow the teacher to choose a variety of modalities to meet the individual needs of the student. Listed below are brief descriptions of the eight modules.

1. Counting Blocks: Three rectangular boxes appear on the screen; inside these are a varying number of colored blocks. The task is to select the correct box that matches the Arabic numeral on the right side of the sreeen. These numerals will range from 1 to 9.

2. Counting Moving Circles: The task is to enter the numeral that corresponds to the number of circles that are "bounced" through a series of ramps to land in a container.

3. Counting Mixed Shapes: Triangles, squares and circles are arranged on the left side of the screen. The object of this module is for the student to count and enter the number of times a particular chosen shape was displayed on the screen.

4. Water Weight: A faucet appears above a water glass. Water fills the glass at varying heights. The student is to enter the unit, indicating the height of water.

5. Comparing Weights: The object of this module is for the student to determine the position where the pans of a two-pan scale will rest based on the number of blocks placed on the pans.

6. Comparing Lengths: The student places a number beneath five vertical bars arranging them from shortest to longest.

7. Simple Addition: Using colored squares, two sets with numbers under them are presented to be added together. These are very simple problems whose sums range between 2 and 9.

8. Simple Subtraction: Problems are presented by using two sets of colored squares with their corresponding numbers printed underneath. The student works the problems whose differences range between 1 and 8.

** *Spelling Bee With Reading Primer*
S.V.E. Microcomputer Software
Edu-Ware Division
Grade level: K - 3
Input System: Keyboard

The program is designed to teach basic reading and spelling concepts. Spelling Bee has three basic learning modes. These modes are as follows:

1. Reading Primer: Creating a bridge between words and the concepts they represent. Reading Primer displays three drawings on the screen and asks the student which drawing represents the same idea as the word on the screen. Using the spacebar and the return key, the student enters the answer.

2. Spelling Bee Drill: The task of this program is for the student to spell correctly the word represented by the drawing on the screen. Letter by letter the word is entered through the keyboard.

3. Spelling Bee Tutorial: A graphic representation shows on the screen and the word is flashed for a predetermined length of time. The student must then type the correct spelling of the word into the computer.

Spelling Bee consists of words selected randomly from twenty-two different word lists. These words are grouped by type from two-to-three letter words, hard C and silent E to assorted words.

This program also has a management mode to allow the teacher access to a student's work, examining the number of attempts and the total number correct.

For physically handicapped students the Reading Primer Mode would be helpful because it allows the student access to the computer with minimal keyboard control.

** *Arcademic Skill Builders in Math*
DLM Computer Education Software
Grade Level: All ages
Input System: Keyboard or game paddles.

Arcademic Skill Builders in Math has a colorful, fast action arcade game format to motivate students to learn fundamental math skills. Providing challenges for students in the four basic math operations and a combination of operations, Arcademic offers six individual titles. They are:

Alien Addition
Minus Mission
Meteor Multiplication
Demolition Division
Alligator Mix- Addition & Subtraction
Dragon Mix- Multiplication and Division

The speed of the drill, the game time, as well as the range of numbers, can be controlled to meet the individual needs of students.

Handicapped students may have difficulty working with these programs because they are very busy and have a great many graphics on the screen at one time.

** *Arcademic Skill Builders in Language Arts*
DLM Computer Education Software
Grade Level: 2 - 6
Input System: Game paddles or keyboard

Vital language arts areas are enhanced through the use of this bright, fun approach to learning. Six individual packages provide drill and practice for students. The areas in the series include:

Word Man—Word building through patterns

Word Invasion—Recognition of six parts of speech

Verb Viper—Subject/verb agreement at four levels

Word Radar—Sight word recognition

Word Master—Antonyms, synonyms and homonyms

Spelling Wiz—Spelling demons

Arcademics provides options in the programs to meet the individual needs of students. The speed at which the game is played and the time per game may be controlled. The level of difficulty of the content can be changed from second grade reading and vocabulary to fourth grade and sound effects may be added or deleted.

The language arts program, like the math program, may be too busy for physically handicapped students.

** *Special Needs—Volume 1*
Minnesota Educational Computing Consortium
Grade Level: 2 and below

Input Method: Input is through multiple choice selections, activited by pressing any key on the keyboard, using the game paddle or an individual switch.

The volume consists of one disk designed to teach spelling words to children with exceptional needs. The disk contains twenty spelling drills. Each drill provides a sentence with three possible answers. A box surrounds the number and moves down over each number. When the student wishes to respond s/he presses the key or paddle. If the answer is correct, it is reinforced; if incorrect, the correct answer is given. Teachers have the option to change words and sentences.

** *Caterpillar*
Minnesota Educational Computing Consortium
Grade Level: Pre-school and grade 1.

Caterpillar is a drill on the upper case alphabet at pre-reading level. It requires the student to type in the missing letter.

** *Train*
Minnesota Educational Computing Consortium
Grade Level: Pre-school and grade 1.

Trains is a drill on the lower case alphabet at pre-reading level. It requires the student to type in the missing letter.

** *A Is For Apple*
Minnesota Educational Computing Consortium
Grade Level: Pre-school and grade 1.

A drill on the initial letter used to spell a pictured word at the prereading level. It requires the student to type in the initial letter.

** *Pictures*
Minnesota Educational Computing Consortium
Grade Level: Pre-school through grade 2.

It is a concentration-type memory game using pictures, and students are asked to type in two letters. Two students can play the game and each must type in her/his name at the beginning of the game.

** *Words*
Minnesota Educational Computing Consortium
Grade Level: K - 2

A concentration-type memory game using words. It requires first grade reading level and the student must type in two letters as well as his/her name at the beginning of the game. It can be played with two players.

** *Shapes*
Minnesota Educational Computing Consortium
Grade Level: Pre-school- 2

A concentration-type memory game using colored geometric shapes. Requires a pre-reading reading level and the student must type in two letters as well as her or his name. Two players can play and a color monitor must be used.

** *Smile*
Minnesota Educational Computing Consortium
Grade Level: Pre-school- 1

A drill on counting identical objects using the numbers 1-9. Prereading ability and typing in one number are required.

** *Wuzzle*
Minnesota Educational Computing Consortium
Grade Level: Pre-school- 1

A drill on counting identical objects in a group of mixed shapes. Pre-reading ability and typing in one number are required.

** *Spaceship*
Minnesota Educational Computing Consortium
Grade Level: K - 1

A drill on addition of two groups of identical objects using sums of 1 through 10. Pre-reading ability and typing in a number which represents the total number of objects is required.

C. Resource Guide to Computer Aids for Handicapped People

The following list of resources give some indication of the rich variety of assistance that is available for handicapped people. New organizations and services not listed may best be located through publications of these we now know about.

Trace Center Registry

A national registry of software for students with special needs. A membership fee of $20 entitles the subscriber to a list of software. For more information write:

Trace Research and Development Center for the Severely Communicatively Handicapped
University of Wisconsin
314 Waisman Center
1500 Highland Avenue
Madison, Wisconsin 53706
Telephone 608/262-6966

Apple Computer Company

Apple will furnish a resource guide to assist in the application of the personal computer for handicapped students. The guide provides a list of people who are willing to provide advice, a bibliography and a summary of work that has been completed for handicapped students.
For a free copy write:

Resource Guide Marketing Service Department
Apple Computer Inc.
10260 Brandley Drive
Cupertino, California 95014

Prentke Romich Company

This firm compiled a review of software for handicapped students published in 1983. A new, computerized service is also being developed called Special Net. Write to:

Prentke Romich
513 Township Road
Shreve, Ohio 44676
Telephone 216/567-2906

The Young People's Logo Association

This is an independent, non-profit, national computer club. They charge a fee of $9 for young people under 18 and a fee of $25 for adults. The club has a library or information on the education of handicapped students. For information contact:

Young People's Logo Association
1208 Hillsdale Drive
Richardson, Texas 75081

The Electronic Information System (EIES)

EIES is an information network and national computer conferencing system. EIES hosts an ongoing conference for exchanging information concerning the handicapped. For more information write:

EIES
New Jersey Institute of Technology
Newark, New Jersey 07102

The Handicapped Educational Exchange (HEX)

HEX was developed to exchange ideas and information to aid handicapped students through the use of advanced technology. HEX is a free, national computer network that can be accessed through a modem or a Telecommunications Device for the Deaf (TDD). Information may be obtained by writing to:

Richard Barth
11523 Charlton Drive
Silver Springs, Maryland 20902

Communications Outlook

This is an international publication that provides the latest developments in computers for use with handicapped students who need assistance with communication. In addition to serving as an information source, Communications Outlook also serves as a reference center for individuals who wish to contact others who are working in the field. For information or subscriptions write to:

Communications Outlook
Artificial Language Laboratory
Computer Science Department
Michigan State University
East Lansing, Michigan 48824
$12 for 4 issues

The Catalyst

This is a bimonthly newsletter published by the Western Center of Microcomputers in Special Education, Inc., a non-profit corporation which provides the latest research related to microcomputers, their development, products and applications for special education use. For a subscription write to:

Western Center for Microcomputers in Special Education
1259 El Camino Real
Suite 275
Menlo Park, California 94025
Institution, Agency or School, $20
Individuals (home address) $12

CHAPTER FOURTEEN
COURSEWARE EVALUATION

There is some good courseware on the market, but educators need to look carefully to locate it. It should be interesting enough so that students who have used microcomputers for years will find it stimulating. We must be concerned not only with today's student who is getting familiar with micros, but also about future students who will have used them for several years. A survey of computer-using teachers indicated courseware should:

Be free of technical or pedagogical errors.

Take advantage of the microcomputer's unique capabilities without substituting flash for substance.

Provide positive reinforcement, and, at the same time, help students to understand wrong answers.

Include some diagnostic and **branching** features.

Be creative, stimulating new perspectives among its users.

Allow for easy teacher modification and provide clearly written support materials and activities.(17)

The following evaluation forms are widely used by teachers for judging software. If you find them too lengthy or in any way inappropriate, edit them to meet your needs.

The staff at the Northwest Regional Educational Laboratory in Portland developed this form after extensive pre-testing with computer-using educators.

MicroSIFT COURSEWARE DESCRIPTION

Title _____
Version
Evaluated_____

Producer _____ Cost_____

Subject/Topics_____

Grade Level(s) (Circle) pre-1 1 2 3 4 5 6 7 8 9 10 11 12 12+

Required Hardware_____

Required Software_____

Software Protected? ___Yes ___No Medium of Transfer: ___Cassette

___ROM Cartridge ___5" Flexible Disk ___8" Flexible Disk

Back Up Policy_____

Producer's field test data is available: ___On Request

___With Package   ___Not Available

MicroSift Form Continued

Instructional Purposes and Techniques
(please check all applicable)

___Remediation ___Standard Instruction ___Enrichment ___Game
___Assessment ___Instructional Management ___Authoring
___Drill and Practice ___Tutorial ___Information Retrieval
___Simulation ___Problem Solving Other_____

Documentation Available
(circle P= program   S= supplementary material)

P S Suggested grade/ability level(s)
P S Instructional objectives
P S Prerequisite skills or activities
P S Sample program output
P S Program operating instructions
P S Pre-test
P S Post-test
P S Teacher's information
P S Resource/reference information
P S Student's instructions
P S Student worksheets
P S Textbook correlation
P S Follow-up activities
P S Other_____

Objectives   ___Stated   ___Inferred

Prerequisites ___Stated   ___Inferred

Describe package Content and Structure, including record keeping
    and reporting functions

The staff at the Northwest Lab has also developed a shorter evaluation form which you may like.

Courseware Evaluation Form

Program Description

Producer:

Version:

Subject:

Required Hardware:

Required Software:

Instructional Techniques:

Documentation Available:

Instructional Objectives:

Instructional Prerequisites:

Content and Structure:

Potential Users:

Major Strengths:

Major Weaknesses:

Courseware Evaluation Form Continued

Evaluation Summary

Rating Categories

SA = Strongly Agree   A = Agree   D = Disagree
SD = Strongly Disagree   NA = Not Applicable

(   ) Content Accuracy
(   ) Educational Value
(   ) Shows No Cultural Stereotyping
(   ) Objectives Well Defined
(   ) Accomplishes Stated Objectives
(   ) Clarity of Content Presentation
(   ) Appropriate Difficulty Level
(   ) Appropriate Graphics/Sound/Color
(   ) Appropriate Motivational Level
(   ) Challenges Student Creativity
(   ) Feedback Effectively Employed
(   ) Student Controls Presentation of Format
(   ) Appropriate Integration With Prior Learning
(   ) Content Can Be Generalized
(   ) Program Comprehensiveness
(   ) Adequate Packaging
(   ) Effective Information Displays
(   ) Clarity of Instructions
(   ) Teacher Facility With Program
(   ) Appropriate Use of Computer Technology
(   ) Program Reliability
(   ) Overall Rating

Ms. Ann Lathrop, Library Coordinator for the San Mateo (California) County Office of Education, has given us permission to reproduce an excellent courseware evaluation form.

CALIFORNIA LIBRARY MEDIA CONSORTIUM FOR CLASSROOM

EVALUATION OF MICROCOMPUTER COURSEWARE
1983 (Revised)

Program Title_____
Title on package/diskette_____
Microcomputer(s) brand/model_____
Memory needed___K Language_____ BASIC(or_____)
Version/copyright date_____ Cost_____
Publisher_____
Peripherals needed:___Disk drive(s)____Cassette
_____Printer Other_____
Other materials/equipment needed_____.
Backup copy available? Yes_____ No_____
Network/Hard Disk Possible? Yes_____ No_____

****

Reviewed by_____
Grade level/subject/position_____
School/District_____
Address/Phone_____

Program Title:_____
Subject Areas:_____
Suggested Grade Levels (circle) K 1 2 3 4 5 6 7 8 9 10 11 12 12+

Type of Program (check all that apply)

___authoring system   ___demonstration
___logic, problem-solving   ___business applications
___drill/practice   ___simulation
___classroom management   ___educational game
___teachers' utility   ___database management
___game   ___testing
___utility   ___word processing
___other:_____

California Library Form Continued

Scope: (check one)

___one or more programs on a single topic
___group of unrelated programs
___one program in an instructional series
___multi-disk curriculum package

Evaluation Criteria

Yes No N/A   General Design:___Excellent ___Good
___Weak   ___Not Acceptable

___ ___ ___   1. Creative, innovative use of computer?
___ ___ ___   2. Effective, appropriate use of computer?
___ ___ ___   3. Follows sound instructional organization?
___ ___ ___   4. Fits well into the curriculum?
___ ___ ___   5. Free of programming errors, problems?

Content: ___Excellent ___Good
___Weak   ___Not Acceptable

___ ___ ___   6. Branches to easier or harder material in
response to student performance?
___ ___ ___   7. Factually correct?
___ ___ ___   8. Free of excessive violence or competition?
___ ___ ___   9. Free of stereotypes-race, ethnic, gender,
age, handicapped?
___ ___ ___   10. Interest, difficulty, typing, and vocabulary
levels are appropriate?
___ ___ ___   11. Modifications of data, speed, word lists, etc.
by instructor are possible?
___ ___ ___   12. Punctuation, spelling, grammar correct?
___ ___ ___   13. Responses to errors are helpful, avoiding
sarcasm or scolding?
___ ___ ___   14. Responses to student success are positive,
enjoyable and appropriate?

Ease of Use: ___Excellent ___Good
___Weak   ___Not Acceptable

California Library Form Continued

_____ 15. Answers may be corrected by user before continuing with program?

_____ 16. Instructions within program are clear, complete, concise?

_____ 17. Instructions can be skipped or recalled to screen?

_____ 18. Instructions on how to end program, start over, are given?

_____ 19. Menu allows user to access specific parts of program?

_____ 20. Paging speed and sequence can be controlled by user?

_____ 21. Screens are neat, attractive, well-spaced?

_____ 22. Sound, if present, is appropriate and may be turned off?

Motivational Devices Used: ___Excellent ___Good
(check all which apply,·   ___Weak   ___Not Acceptable
 ratings and approaches)

___graphics for instruction ___graphics for reward ___color
___scoring ___game format ___random order ___sound ___timing
___personalization

Documentation: ___Excellent ___Good
(check all available,   ___Weak   ___Not Acceptable
 ratings and types)

___none ___instruction manual ___teacher's guide ___tests
___instructions appear on screen ___instructional objectives
___suggested classroom activities ___workbook
___student worksheets

Overall Opinion:

___Great program. I recommend it highly!
___Pretty good, useful.
___OK, but you might wait for a better one.
___Would select only if modifications were made.
___Not useful.

California Library Form Continued

Describe content and main objectives of this program:

In your opinion, were the objectives met?

*   What classroom management, testing, or performance reporting is provided?

How many students/classes can be managed by this program?

Is the management system easy to use?

*   Describe any special strengths of program:

*   Comments/concerns/questions:

*   Comments comparing with other programs which are similar:

*   Suggestions to the author/publisher:

Briefly Describe Students and Their Response to Program

Grade levels where used:_____Subject:_____

Behavior observed that indicates learning took place:

Other reactions:

Any problems experienced?

Any quotes you want to share?

Irene and Owen Thomas of Laguna Beach, California, have given us permission to reproduce a short evaluation form which many teachers find helpful.

Evaluating Microcomputer Courseware

1. Content

Accurate, valuable, non-sexist, explicitly defined goals.
Yes( ) ?( ) No( )

2. Level of Difficulty

Appropriate means of response (not all multiple choice), recognition of attention span, branching to remedial subroutines or tutorials.
Yes( ) ?( ) No( )

3. Technical Aspects

Graphics, sound, color (do they enhance rather than distract?), appropriate use of humor, personal style, variety of response.
Yes( ) ?( ) No( )

4. Challenge to Creativity

Student involvement (active rather than passive), user (teacher) control over input variables, some open-ended questions, encouragement of creative uses of knowledge acquired.
Yes( ) ?( ) No( )

5. Feedback

Credible, timely, quantitative, explanations of why particular responses are incorrect, selection of material relative to past performance.
Yes( ) ?( ) No( )

6. Applicability
    Opportunities to apply skills in generalized (non-computer) situations, organization that lends itself to transfer of acquired skills.
    Yes( )   ?( )   No( )

7. Support Materials

    Pre-instruction materials, worksheets and other follow-up, teachers' guides.
    Yes( )   ?( )   No( )

8. Operation

    Management programs (not requiring external paper documentation), options for returning to starting point, options for moving to another section, accurate evaluation of performance, unambiguous instructions, minimum teacher supervision.
    Yes( )   ?( )   No( )

    Could the user get lost with no way out?
    Yes( )   ?( )   No( )

    Could the material be more effectively taught by other means?
    Yes( )   ?( )   No( )

    Is the program merely a textbook/workbook displayed on a screen (or does it make effective use of a computer's unique capabilities)?
    Yes( )   ?( )   No( )

If you don't like a program, tell the salesperson/ distributor/ publisher why--as specifically as you can. This is the most effective way of getting programs you will like.

Here is another short form you may find useful.

How to Evaluate Educational Courseware

DOES THE PROGRAM RUN ?
* Check the program from the beginning to the end.
* Try some "wrong" answers.

IS THE PROGRAM EASY TO USE ?
* Are adequate instructions given on the screen?
* Are screen formats consistent throughout the software?

IS THE ACTIVITY EDUCATIONALLY SOUND ?
* Is the presented activity appropriate to and integrated into the concepts to be taught?
* Is the activity appropriate for the age of the student?
* Are the called-for responses reasonable tasks?
* Does the computer enhance this activity, or is the activity more suited to another medium, such as print or film?
* Is the program attractive and interesting?

WHO IS IN CONTROL---STUDENT OR MACHINE?
* Does the student determine the pace of instruction?
* Does the student have sufficient time to read all the information on the screen?

DOES THE PROGRAM PRESENT THE CONCEPT TO BE LEARNED IN A HARMONIOUS AND WELL BALANCED WAY?
* Each element should support and reinforce other elements.
* Graphics should support and reinforce objectives of the program.
* Sound should be used to advantage and should not be distracting.

We turn now to a set of courseware criteria that may be helpful from *The Book of Apple Computer Software.* (18)

1. Ease of Use   Are the screen layouts (or documentation) clear so the user can "run" the program with a minimum of difficulty?
2. Documentation   Does it answer all the questions; is it clear; is it sufficiently extensive?
3. Reliability   Does the program do what it is supposed to do?
4. Price/Usefulness Ratio   This means: is the buyer getting value for his money? For example, a fair program from one vendor priced at $7.95 might be a better value than a slightly better program of the same type from another vendor priced at $24.95.
5. Vendor Support   Does the software company back its products? Are they available to answer questions? Will they replace a program that is defective?
6. Visual Appeal   Does the program take advantage of the graphic capabilities of your computer?
7. Error Handling   Does the program "bomb" during execution? Are there proper "error trapping" routines?
8. Creativity   Is the program creative and imaginative?
9. Challenge   Does the program have sufficient challenge for the intended audience?
10. Copyable   Is it possible to make (back-up) copies if needed?
11. Availability   Can the program be obtained when needed?
12. Educational Merit   Most important, is the program educationally sound?

The following is a sample review applying the criteria. The point scale is an average of the various scores using the following ratings:

10-20 Unacceptable
21-40 Poor
41-60 Fair
61-80 Good
Math Tutor   Retail $7.95
Company: Instant Software
Language: Applesoft and Integer

Ease of Use	80	Documentation	85
Reliability	90	Vendor Support	70
Price/Usefulness	85	Error Handling	90
Visual Appeal	75	Educ Merit	70
Creativity	70	Challenge	80
Copyable	95	Availability	85

This Low Resolution program provides math practice for children while playing a game with the following three programs: HANGING A program that presents addition, substraction, multiplication or division of decimals. As you answer the problems correctly, the hangman moves down the steps avoiding the noose. SPELLBINDER As you add, subtract, multiply and divide fractions, you are a magician competing against another magician controlled by the computer. If you answer the problems correctly, you try to cast a spell on your opponent. If you miss a problem, the positions are reversed. Both you and the scorer start the competition with 20 points. If either reaches zero he loses. WHOLESPACE The program requires addition, substraction, multiplication or division of whole numbers. You pilot your spaceship as you lead the attack on the enemy planet. You can move your ship only if you answer the problem correctly. If you answer incorrectly, the enemy fires on you.

All the programs have varying levels of difficulty and a choice of attempts to answer correctly. The chance to play games while being tutored is appealing. It would be more effective in High Resolution.

This is a useful review and we expect to see more books and other publications of courseware reviews coming on to the market each year as the market of potential purchasers increases. One that has promise is *The Digest of Software Reviews: Education* published by School and Home Courseware, Inc., 1341 Bulldog Lane, Fresno, California 93710.

DISTRICT ADAPTATIONS

We encourage districts to use these forms in whatever manner works best for their unique situation. To accomplish this, several districts have changed the forms in the following manner.

A medium sized surburban district uses the California Library Media Consortium for Classroom Evaluation form by eliminating the last section and focusing upon the numbered items. A large, urban district plans to change the format of the MicroSIFT Courseware Description by arranging all items in even columns rather than the mixture of rows and columns seen in this chapter.

A small district selected items from several instruments, including those in this chapter, to create their own instrument. Another small district uses the California Library Media Consortium instrument in combination with one developed at a nearby university which focuses upon Program Utility (5 items); Technical Characteristics (12 items); Curriculum (4 Items) and Instruction (5 items).

Perhaps the important consideration is to use an instrument that is curriculum oriented, easy to use and one that gets the teacher to consider whether the courseware is in fact meeting her/his teaching objectives. In our experience it is common for district specialists to use a long and somewhat complex instrument such as the MicroSIFT form and for classroom teachers to use a brief instrument such as the one titled Evaluating Microcomputer Courseware in this chapter.

CHAPTER FIFTEEN
ADMINISTRATIVE APPLICATIONS FOR THE COMPUTER

Educators have a significant amount of record-keeping and paper work that needs to be completed, and much of it is in the form of reports which use the same format repeatedly. This is an ideal situation for computer utilization if the administrator has the right software to do the job.

General application programs for administrative use fall into four categories:

1. Word Processing;
2. Data Base Management Systems;
3. Electronic Spread Sheets; and
4. Budgeting, Accounting and other Business Management

WORD PROCESSING

Word processing on the computer can turn a laborious, time-consuming task into one that is easy once the user has a word processing program that works at her or his level. If you are a beginner, begin with a program with few commands and move to a more sophisticated one later as your skills increase. Word processing programs are most helpful when a good deal of writing and re-writing must be done. With the assistance of the program the user turns the computer into an electronic pencil, paper and eraser. In a matter of seconds the word processor can help edit sentences or paragraphs by means of deletion, substitution or rearrangement. Programs for correcting spelling errors and typographical errors are also available.

The word processor for school use is an effective tool for customizing letters to parents, completing state and federal applications, and creating forms for routine use within your school. Many of these documents, once copied on to a disk and saved, can be updated with minor changes in a short period of time.

The most difficult task is not using the programs but, rather, selecting the right ones to use in the beginning. The following programs are word processing programs commonly used in schools.

* Bank Street Writer or Milliken Word Processor

    These are two of the simplest word processing programs. They have a limited number of commands, which means you can start right out and make them do what you want in a few minutes. You may find they will serve your needs well and you will never need a more sophisticated program. Try not to be influenced by others who have more experience with computers who may scoff at the use of these "children's" programs.

* Apple Writer II

    A widely used program of medium complexity, it can turn the computer into a text editor. Writing, revising, editing and printing letters, reports and other documents can be accomplished quickly and inexpensively. Some people find it a bit difficult to keep the commands in mind for Apple Writer II, especially if it is not used very often.

Customizing Letters to Parents

* Word Star

The sophisticated user's favorite, this full capacity program offers many special features. These include margin adjustment on the side of the screen, the ability to edit a document while printing out another, and the capability to insert new information easily. Some of our students who have compared Apple Writer II and Word Star find Word Star easier to use because one can have the most-used commands at the top of the page while writing. It is an expensive program, as one would expect.

Other software worthy of consideration includes Benchmark by Metasoft; Scripsit by Tandy-Radio Shack; and Word Pro 4 Plus by Professional Software.

DATA BASE MANAGEMENT SYSTEMS

These are systems of electronic filing which will be helpful in maintaining files and records. The potential of a data base management system is hard to comprehend at first because it can do so many tasks you won't think of until you learn to use it. Such a system can be used to keep track of special program students, bilingual students, busing, free or reduced lunch recipients, immunization records, and discipline referrals, just to list a few common uses. A data base system also centralizes record-keeping and frees up space for other purposes in crowded school offices.

The most important factor in selecting a data base management system is the number of records that are involved. Small-scale systems will hold between 800-1600 records, depending on the number of fields used in each file. The information in the file for a small-scale system is stored on a **floppy disk**.

A data base management system offers the user the ability to scan, retrieve, maintain, delete and print out a report combining any or all of the information that is stored in the system with relative ease. The small-scale systems are easy to use and thus a beginner can operate them.

The following programs are among the most widely used.

* VisiFile

VisiFile has the power to provide multiple indexes into a file. Its special features include the capability to create new files; change the structure of existing files; add, delete and change existing data; perform calculations with numeric information; set up a format of fields that will be seen on the screen; print reports; mail labels; and transfer information from one VisiCorp (the publisher) program to another.

The VisiFile program is quite easy to learn to use. The program displays instructions on the screen, leading the user step by step in setting up and maintaining files. If there is any doubt about what to do, a comprehensive manual comes with the program, serving as a tutorial for use and as a reference guide. We find it to be one of the best programs available.

* File Cabinet

A small-scale filing system from Apple with limited scope, File Cabinet does not allow the transfer of information from one file to another as VisiFile does. It is designed for the user with little or no knowledge of computers. It is slow and sometimes difficult to operate.

* D B Master

This is a flexible, fast system, capable of handling larger files and, for some, easy to use. It uses a system called "Dynamic Prompting" which provides a list of variable options the user may need, thus eliminating the need for memorization. File lengths are limited on D B Master and some have found the program confusing in places.

* Personal Filing System

A simple, flexible program that works well for the beginner. It offers the user the ability to create files, record, retrieve and review information swiftly. It gives the user freedom to arrange information to meet individual needs and provides the capability to change a form without having to reenter information already stored. It is compatible with other software available such as PFS Report from Software Publishing.

It might also be worthwhile to explore dBase II published by Ashton-Tate as an option.

ELECTRONIC SPREAD SHEETS

These are used when extensive and repetitive calculations are needed. Rows and columns provide a two-dimensional table where a change in a single value will cause all other data to be corrected immediately. Thus if one is estimating the effect of a pay raise for teachers in a district, there can be instant comparison of 5%, 6% and 7%, for example. The capabilities offered by spreadsheets make budgeting, tracking attendance, financial projections, or enrollment projections a matter of a few minutes rather than days of work.

* VisiCalc

This is the best selling piece of software on the market in any category. A 48 K (old Apple II) system may not contain sufficient memory for some VisiCalc applications. In these cases you would purchase a Language Card with an additional 16 K of memory to increase the memory for your microcomputer. VisiCalc will carry out all of the calculations listed above and many more highly specialized ones as well. It can serve as a powerful planning and forecasting tool for large organizations. The problem is not what it can do but when to use it. Typically, it should only be used where extensive calculations are involved.

The program does take a great deal of time to learn to use if you are working your way through the manual in a step-by-step fashion. Pelican Press of Laguna, P.O. Box 4003, Laguna Beach, California 92652, offers a 10-page "short course" and training disk which teaches one about 70% of the VisiCalc commands in a few hours, depending upon user experience. The program is called VisiCalc Essentials. It can be used as an individual tutorial or as the basis for inservice at the school or district level.

Other programs to consider include Multiplan by Microsoft and Supercalc by Sorcim. We are aware of organizations where VisiCalc has been replaced by Supercalc.

BUDGETING, ACCOUNTING AND OTHER BUSINESS MANAGEMENT PROGRAMS

We have not personally used the following programs but we know of school systems that do. We have heard positive remarks about Activity Accountant by Scott-Foresman; Budget by Commodore; Budgetary Control and Planning by E.D.I.S.; Budget Officer by Educational Microcomputer Associates; Budget System-Educational Institutions by Commodore Bursar by Addison-Wesley; Cafeteria Management by E.D.I.S.; Internal Accounting System by Educational Performance Systems; Project Planning and Budgeting by Charles Mann and Associates; Purchase by Addison-Wesley; and Student Billing System by School Management Systems.

In the personnel area you might consider ESM-100 by Educational Software and Marketing; Personnel Data Recorder by Scott-Foresman; Personnel and Skills Inventory, Position Control and Staff Development, all by Mega Systems; and Teacher File by the Pasco (Florida) School District.

SPECIALIZED PROGRAMS

In addition to the application programs mentioned, we would like to identify two that are highly specialized. These are Spell Star and Mail Merge. Both programs are used in conjunction with Word Star.

Spell Star is designed to locate misspelled words and typographical errors. It contains a standard "dictionary" of 20,000 commonly used words and you add to it additional words you use frequently. It then lists misspelled words and typographical errors for you to correct. The program is especially useful for persons who are not good at spelling and proofreading. If you rarely make mistakes, it is not worth the time it takes to run it.

Mail Merge is a program to perform mass mailing tasks for you, such as sending a letter to all parents. It will create and store labels as well as reproduce letters. Letters can be individualized with appropriate addresses included on them and the mailing envelope. This is a valuable piece of software and it, or an equivalent program, probably should be part of every school's software collection.

In summary, there are a variety of software application programs available to help administrators get much of the basic work of the school office accomplished. In each category there are simple, inexpensive programs to use when one is inexperienced, as well as more sophisticated programs for later use. It is critical to find secretarial helpers who are willing to learn these time-saving skills. We have heard, for example, that in one organization, use of the word processor eliminated one half a secretarial position for each word processor purchased.

Our Apple II+ word processing system that we used to write this book cost us $800 for the Apple II+, $600 for the two disk drives, $400 for the hardware package to convert the Apple so it can run Word Star, $100 for the monitor, and $600 for the letter quality Comrex printer—a fine system for about $2500. If computers follow the same cycle that calculators did, they should drop in price about 10% each year and, at the same time, offer greater performance.

There are three rules to keep in mind when using administrative software.

1. Use the computer primarily where there is repetition.
2. When using numeric data, use the computer where you are having the most problems or where there is an obvious application such as in salary projections.
3. Try to scale down data base applications such as recording test results for each student.

The computer will never get tired, but your staff will, and if data is not entered in a timely fashion, you will miss many of your best opportunities to take advantage of the computer's capabilities.

CHAPTER SIXTEEN
A MODEL FOR INTRODUCING MICROCOMPUTERS

A significant number of teachers have a negative view of computers; to them technology seems cold and impersonal. They teach because they want warm, personal relationships with students and they are not going to diminish good interaction with students to gain the advantageous use of micro-computers. We have great sympathy for this view which we held in past years. Then we had the good fortune to be introduced to micros in a faculty work room at the University of Maryland.

The work room was carpeted, had pleasant draperies, wooden tables for the computers, and floor lamps. It was quite a contrast to the typical computer room with tile floors, neon lights and metal desks. If you want many of your teachers to use micros, you might consider putting them in a room that is more like a faculty lounge than a sterile laboratory. This is but one example of the "hi-touch" concept that *Megatrends* author John Naisbitt has identified for us.(19) Technology must fit into our lives in a manner that is consistent with our values or we will not embrace it.

The planning model which follows was developed by Joel Shawn of the Los Angeles County Superintendent of Schools Office. It offers some excellent suggestions for introducing microcomputer technology into a school.

Step 1: The district, school or educational organization decides to explore the use of microcomputers. This happens in response to a variety of change agents. For example, a member of the district board may own a microcomputer. Teachers within the district may have purchased their own computers and brought them to school. A neighboring local district may be actively involved with the use of microcomputers.

Step 2: The school board forms a microcomputer steering committee or task force with a mandate to create a district or school-wide plan for the use of microcomputers. This group should be made up of representative individuals from all constituent groups. In addition, a needs validation should be done to insure the use of microcomputers is a priority item.

Step 3: The task force, school board, and other individuals who represent district or school leadership receive awareness level microcomputer training. The goal of this training is to provide a skill level which will enable the individuals to make decisions.

Step 4A: The task force does a curriculum review to determine strand areas and specific educational objectives which will be linked to the use of micro-computers. The task force additionally determines if a computer literacy strand is to be incorporated into the curriculum.

Step 4B: The task force does a review of district and/or school business operations to determine appropriate tasks which would be related to the business use of microcomputers.

Step 5: The task force reviews existing software to select programs to accomplish goals established in steps 4A and 4B. If software is not found, a process for development of programs is created.

Step 6: The task force reviews and recommends microcomputer hardware to support software needs identified in Step 5.

Step 7: The task force writes district or school-wide microcomputer infusion

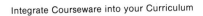

Integrate Courseware into your Curriculum

plan. This plan will include major goals, timelines, training requirements, and budget needs. The plan should be in a three-to five-year time frame.

Step 8: The task force presents infusion plan to district office for approval and implementation.(20)

The key factor in this approach is the effort to connect planning for the introduction of microcomputers with your ongoing curriculum development process. In other words, build your microcomputer curriculum into the established curriculum so that it will not be perceived as a temporary appendage. It should also save you money in purchasing courseware, as a careful review process of courseware helps preclude inappropriate courseware purchases.

CHAPTER SEVENTEEN
INSERVICE TRAINING FOR USING MICROCOMPUTERS

Computers are moving into the school setting so rapidly in some districts that this new technology may cause fear on the part of staff who imagine they will not be able to learn the skills required to use microcomputers. If such fears are to be reduced, an inservice program should be developed to provide a minimal level of computer literacy for all staff.

Arthur Luehrmann of Computer Literacy, a Berkeley, California firm, sees five aspects to computer literacy:

1. Students should know the mechanics of using a computer, including how to turn it on, and load and run a software program.
2. They should know how to write a simple program, just as they should be able to write a short letter.
3. They should know some BASIC, the most widely used computer language.
4. They should become familiar enough with the computer to view it as a tool and not be afraid of it. In addition they should have an understanding of the social and ethical issues involved in using a computer.
5. They should be able to solve problems that interest them with the computer, to tell the computer to do the things they want it to do. (22)

Our own list would differ from Luehrmann's on points 2 and 3. For us, on point 2 it seems more important to be able to locate software that will accomplish tasks we face in our work than it is to be able to program. In point 3, we would have students develop a practical mastery of the commands in a general applications software program that seems relevant to them, such as a word processing program like Apple Writer II or Word Star.

Like all level of literacy questions, this one should be answered for each school district after considerable debate where teachers, administrators, computer experts, students, parents and community members all have an opportunity for input.

In a practical sense, one of the key factors governing the curriculum will be the views of the individual(s) who provide the instruction. For example, many districts require trainers from the firm where they purchase their microcomputers to offer computer literacy training to a cadre of interested teachers as part of the purchase agreement. These teachers are then identified as computer coordinators who return to their individual schools to train other teachers on site.

Whatever the content of computer literacy for teachers, administrators and students, and it probably will be different for each group, the inservice needs to be a "hands on the computer" experience. Trainees should be able to turn on the computer; load, run and copy programs; initialize disks; and review software to find what they need. These skills will enable the users to become more comfortable with the computer and begin to dispel fears and misunderstandings.

When we make presentations on computer utilization in school districts, we stress the notion that the greatest use of the computer is going to be for word processing, not mathematical calculations. Thus it makes sense that the teacher in charge of inservice should be from a humanities or social studies background. The most computer literate teachers are typically from mathematics backgrounds and they tend to emphasize mathematics and science in their approaches, often causing the English teachers to back away from learning about computers. A nice compromise is to have the non-math teacher be in charge and the math teacher(s) as expert consultants. Certainly the math teachers' capabilities should be utilized.

In setting up the inservice training, each person should have his or her own micro to practice on, or at most two people could share a computer. The "hands on" experience is critical in building computer skills.

The following outline of a computer literacy inservice for teachers using the Apple II is one which has been successful in the schools in Fullerton, California.(23) We will present several inservice models for you to use "as is" or to adapt to your situation.

School Computer Coordinator Training
Session 1

I. Review of Computer Coordinator Survey
   A. Scoring on pretest
   B. Prior experience
II. Major Components in a Computer
   A. Input
   Keyboards, paddles, graphics tablets, and lightpens
   B. Processing
   CPU (6502 in Apple)
   C. Memory
   RAM, ROM, disk drives, cassette tape recorders and hard disks
   D. Output
   Video screen, printers, and plotters
   E. Miscellaneous Components
   Power supply, RF modulators, cassette in/out jacks, line cord, expansion
   slots, interface cards, game I/O connectors
III. Connecting and Adjusting the System
   A. Be careful mating plugs to sockets
   B. Static electricity—how to discharge it and why
IV. Homework
   A. Keyboard program—go run it if you have never done so before.

School Computer Coordinator Training
Session 2

I. Programming
  A. What is a program?
  B. What are computer languages?

II. Higher Level Languages
  A. Higher than what?
  B. Examples:
    BASIC—Beginner's All-purpose Symbolic Instruction Code
    Others—LOGO, FORTRAN, COBOL, Pascal, Forth and Assembly

III. Immediate Execution Commands
  A. HOME
  B. PRINT

PWIV. Deferred Execution Commands
  A. Use of line numbers
  B. Use of LIST
  C. Use of NEW
  D. Writing a program

V. Disk Operations
  A. CATALOG
  B. LOAD
  C. RUN "program"
  D. DELETE
  E. SAVE
  F. LOCK

VI. Error Messages
  A. SYNTAX ERROR
  B. EXTRA IGNORED
  C. FILE NOT FOUND (DOS)

VII. Use of the Manuals
  A. Become familiar with the DOS manual. It lists all directions for initializing disks, as well as using a variety of utility programs on the System Master Disk. DOS error messages are also explained.
  B. The Applesoft Reference Manual lists Applesoft error messages. This can be helpful when you don't understand what the computer is trying to tell you.

VIII. Homework
  A. Using the directions given to you, initialize the disk that you were given at the last session. You may use the Hello program listed in the handout if you like.
  B. Type in the Sample Program listing on the handout titled "Entering a Program from a Listing." Then SAVE it on your newly initialized disk. RUN it to make sure it works.

Handout 1: How to Initialize a Disk

1. Use another initialized DOS 3.3 disk or the System Master disk to "boot" or make the program ready to run.
2. Type HOME to clear the screen.
3. Type NEW to clear the computer's memory.
4. Type in your "Hello" program. This will be the program that will automatically be run each time this disk is "booted." A sample "Hello" program is seen as Handout 2 below.
5. RUN your "Hello" program to make sure it works as you had planned.
6. Now put the disk to be initialized in the disk drive.
7. After making sure the right disk is in the drive, type INIT HELLO. The disk drive will begin running, and initialization will be complete in about 60 seconds.
8. Note that initializing erases all previous information recorded on the disk. Be sure that the correct disk is in the drive before typing INIT HELLO.

Handout 2: Sample HELLO Program

```
10 HOME
20 PRINT "DISK INITIALIZED ON JUNE 7, 1983"
30 PRINT
40 PRINT "BY YOUR NAME"
50 END
```

Handout 3: Entering a Program From a Listing

1. Turn on the computer with the System Master or other initialized disk in the disk drive.
2. After the disk has finished "booting," type HOME to clear the screen.
3. Type NEW to remove any program from the computer's memory. This allows you to start with a "clean slate".
4. Type in the program listing, typing it *exactly* as listed.
5. When done, type LIST to review your program. If errors are detected, retype the line numbers affected. The old line will be automatically removed. To remove an unwanted line, just type the line's number and it will be removed.
6. Test your program by typing RUN. Your program should now execute properly. If errors are noted, list the lines indicated and repair the errors.
7. If all is well, make sure that the disk on which you want to save the program is in the disk drive. Type SAVE (program name) to save the program on the disk. (Program name) should be the name that you want to use for your program.

Handout 4: Sample Program Listing

Try entering the listing below following the procedures outlined above. See if you can guess what the program will do before you run it.

```
100 REM FIRST PROGRAM LISTING
110 HOME
120 PRINT "PLEASE TYPE YOUR FIRST AND LAST NAMES."
130 PRINT
140 PRINT
150 INPUT "    "; NAMES$
160 FOR I = 1 TO LEN (NAMES$)
170 PRINT LEFT$ (NAME$,I)
180 NEXT I
190 PRINT
200 PRINT "WASN'T THAT FUN?"
```

School Computer Coordinator Training

Session 3

 I. Review of previous sessions: What you should be aware of now
   A. Major parts of a computer
   B. Hardware cautions—static electricity
   C. Disk cautions—magnetic fields and heat
   D. The computer keyboard
   E. Definition of a program and a programming language
   F. How to insert a disk and turn on the computer
   G. How to type responses to questions that appear on the screen
   H. Some of the uses of the computer
 II. Classification of software
   A. Outline of varieties of software
   B. These are examples only. This is not an all-inclusive list.
 III. Miscellaneous questions and issues
 IV. Home work
   Go into a computer store and browse. Look through several magazines and books. If you see anything interesting, ask the salesperson for a demonstration.

An Introductory Inservice for Educators

Markley Morrill, a computer using teacher in the Santa Ana Unified School District, Santa Ana, California has written a fine inservice training program which does not emphasize programming skills. It covers Hardware Basics, Software Basics, Teacher Utilities, Teacher Management Software and Instructional Software and Software Evaluation.

Session 1: Hardware Basics

Objective: At the end of this session the participant will be able to . . .
. . . list name and function of the main components of a microcomputer.
. . . load, catalog and run computer software.
. . . prepare the printer for operation.

Instructional Sequence:

1. Identify each major component of the microcomputer and explain its function.
2. If possible, open up and display the inside of the computer. Explain the basic parts.
3. Step through the process of loading a disk, requesting a catalog and calling up a program.
4. Step through the sequence of preparing the printer for operation.

Activities:

1. Allow participants an opportunity to insert and remove the cards inside the computer.
2. Allow participants to load, catalog and run several sample programs. If possible, let participants run a self-directed program that teaches one the keyboard.
3. Allow participants to prepare a printer for operation and print some text and/or graphics.

Materials:

—printed materials detailing parts and their function in the computer; instructions for loading a disk, running a program and operating the printer.

—suitable sample programs.

Session 2: Software Basics

Objective: At the end of this session the participant will be able to..
 . . . categorize the different types of educational software.
 . . . make backup copies of unprotected disks.
 . . . list the major factors in software evaluation.

Instructional Sequence:

1. Briefly review the major concepts covered in the previous session.
2. Explain the difference between the major types of educational software (instruction, utilities and management). Add a comment that this inservice will examine each of the three types in the following sessions. Provide a brief demonstration of each type, if possible.
3. Explain the difference between protected, unprotected and public domain software. Demonstrate how to copy public domain software and to erase disks so they can reused.
4. Give out one or more types of software evaluation forms. Explain the major factors to consider in software evaluation. Discuss the importance of such evaluation.

Activities:

1. Allow participants an opportunity to copy public domain software. Explain how to copy a backup copy of a protected program where this is possible.
2. As a group, evaluate a piece of educational software using an evaluation instrument(s).

Materials:

—printed material detailing disk copying routine.

—printed software evaluation forms.

—protected and public domain disks.

—disk with copy program such as DOS 3.3 System Master for Apple

Session 3: Software-Teacher Utilities

Objective: At the end of this session the participant will be able to . . .
. . . define what a teacher utility is.
. . . produce a student worksheet using one of the teacher utilities.

Instructional Sequence:

1. Define what a teacher utility is. Give examples of teacher utilities such as crossword puzzle maker, poster maker, banner maker, word-find designer, test generator and word processor.
2. Demonstrate a variety of teacher utilities.

Activities:

1. Allow participants to use and produce their own materials for classroom use with the teacher utilities software such as that available from the Minnesota Educational Computing Consortium.

Material:

—printed material detailing use of the utilities.

—a variety of utility programs.

Session 4: Teacher Management Software

Objective: At the end of this session the participant will be able to . . .
 . . . define what a management program does.
 . . . use several management programs.

Instructional Sequence:

1. Define what management software is and indicate how it can assist teachers. Give examples of useful teacher management programs such as grade recording, grade analysis and reporting, data base management, and, if time allows, an electronic spreadsheet program.
2. Demonstrate a variety of the teacher management programs.

Activities:

Allow the teachers to practice running programs. Have teachers set up and load files, practice calling up files, revise information in files, insert new material into files and print out all and part of a file.

Materials:

—printed materials summarizing how to use each teacher management program you wish to emphasize.

—printed material showing previous use of the management programs as they were printed out and necessary program disks.

Session 5: Instructional Software and Software Evaluation

Objective: At the end of this session the participant will be able to . . .
. . . list the types of instructional programs available.
. . . evaluate instructional programs suitable for the teacher's grade level and/or subject area.

Instructional Sequence:

1. Define the goal of instructional programs and indicate how different program types seek to achieve their goals (ie. drill and practice, tutorials, games and simulations).
2. Demonstrate each type of instructional program, preferably in different subjects and/or at different grade levels.

Activities:

1. Allow participants to compare a variety of instructional programs of differing types at different grade levels and in a variety of subjects.
2. Use the software evaluation instruments previously discussed to evaluate several programs. Ask the teachers to select an instrument that teachers at their school would be willing to use.

Materials:

—printed materials summarizing types of instructional software.

—software evaluation forms.

—a variety of instructional programs to evaluate.

Carefully Selected Courseware Keeps Student Interest High

CHAPTER EIGHTEEN
A COMPUTER SKILLS CONTINUUM

The Irvine Unified School District, Irvine, California, has developed a computer skills continuum which may be useful as a basis for discussion as you create your district continuum.(24) This continuum assumes availability of microcomputers from K through grade 12. Adjustments should be made according to the grade your students begin to use the computer.

Grade: Kindergarten

1. Identify parts of a computer.
2. Use a prepared program in a microcomputer.
3. Identify and use the keyboard letters and numbers.
4. Demonstrate proper care of hardware and software.
5. Demonstrate awareness of computer use in everyday life.
6. Develop computer vocabulary.
   - a. Hardware
   - b. Software
   - c. Keyboard
   - d. Disk Drive
   - e. Monitor
   - f. Diskette
   - g. Program

7. Describe a computer and how it works in simple terms.
8. Write simple procedures in LOGO.
9. Create graphic designs.
10. Use Turtle graphics to make shapes.

Grade: First

1. Understand computer terms.
2. Use appropriate terms when talking about computers.
3. Explain how a computer works (input and output).
4. Understand implications of copyright laws.
5. Identify and use common special purpose keys.
6. Demonstrate how to insert a disk, turn on the computer and boot up a program.
7. Recognize simple error messages such as "syntax error" or "break in."
8. Explain simple error messages.
9. Understand some of the things a computer can do.
10. Use relative and absolute coordinates in a graphics program.
11. List different computer languages and their uses.
12. Write procedures with single and multiple inputs.
13. Use the keyboard.
14. Move shapes using Turtle Graphics.

Grade: Second

1. Define hardware and software.
2. Run a program from the catalog on a menu.
3. Use and interact with a drill and practice program.
4. Describe standard flow-chart symbols.
5. Read a flow-chart.
6. Explain the concept of programming in simple terms.
7. Apply problem-solving strategies using a computer program.
8. Understand some advantages and disadvantages in using a computer.
9. Explain everyday applications of computers.
10. Identify computer-related occupations.
11. Explain how computers affect our lives.
12. Identify several everyday applications of computers.
13. Talk about our future and the computer.
14. Do rotations using Turtle Graphics.
15. Use LOGO at a simple level.

Grade: Third

1. Recognize capabilities of different computer types (sizes, brands and special purpose machines).
2. Describe common uses of computers.
3. Develop correct keyboarding skills.
4. Demonstrate ability to stop, escape from and continue a program as needed.
5. Use and interact with a simulation program.
6. Use DOS commands to save a simple program.
7. Use editing procedure to correct programs.
8. Develop and apply strategies for debugging programs.

9. History of computers.
10. Use of logic in computer operations.
11. How a computer works.
12. Parts of a computer.
13. LOGO programming.
14. Problem solving with LOGO.

Grade: Fourth

1. List characteristics of each generation of computers.
2. Identify and read computer-related books and magazines.
3. Write a three-step flow chart to represent a solution to a task.
4. Identify ways computers are used to help consumers (social studies).
5. Illustrate the importance of the computer in modern science and industry (social studies).
6. Identify career fields related to computer development and use (social studies).
7. Describe the historical development of computing devices as related to other scientific devices.
8. Differentiate among micro, mini and main frame computers.
9. Identify the five major components of a computer.
10. Define "input" and "output" and give an example of each.
11. State what will happen if instructions are not properly stated in precise language for each computer type.
12. Describe several standard flow chart symbols.
13. Draw a flow chart to represent a solution to a proposed problem.
14. Use the computer to accomplish a mathematical task (mathematics).
15. Define binary numbers; give an example.
16. Define hardware; give an example.
17. Define software; give an example.

Grade: Fifth

1. List values of computer skills for future employment.
2. Describe serious legal issues resulting from widespread computer use.
3. Use and interact with a problem-solving program.
4. Use a computer as a word processor.
5. Copy a simple program.
6. Delete all or part of a program.
7. Translate a simple flow chart into a computer program.
8. Modify existing programs.
9. Identify several computer generations.
10. Run a "counter" program.
11. In BASIC use the "if then" command.
12. In BASIC use the "on—go to" command.
13. In BASIC use the "read data" command.
14. Write and edit a paragraph with the word processor.

Grade: Sixth

1. Explain the statement "Computer mistakes are mistakes by people."
2. Describe the impact of computers in a social, political and environmental sense.
3. Recognize variations in the impact of computers on different people.
4. Explain the meaning of "word processing."
5. Explain what is meant by different computer "types."
6. Briefly describe two computer languages.
7. Explain the term "data handling."
8. Explain the term "looping."
9. In BASIC use the "for-next" command.
10. In BASIC use the "random number" command.
11. Using BASIC, create a simple-problem solving program.
12. Using a graphics program, create a headline for a story.

Grade: Seventh

1. Hypothesize about the limitations of computers.
2. Identify advantages and dangers of computer data bases.
3. Use a data base program.
4. Use an electronic spreadsheet program such as VisiCalc.
5. Use a utility program that is used at your school frequently.
6. Distinguish random computer commands from a computer program.
7. List several fundamental statements and commands for your computer.
8. Distinguish system commands from program statements.
9. Write a simple program in text and graphics.
10. Write a simple program to accomplish a specific task in BASIC.
11. Define the term "data base" and its use in various careers (social studies).
12. State the value of computer skills for future employment (social studies).
13. Describe problems related to "invasion of privacy" (social studies).
14. Describe advantages and disadvantages of a data base of personal information (social studies).
15. Describe ways computers are used to commit crimes and how these crimes are detected.
16. Describe how computers are used by social scientists (social studies).
17. Identify ways in which computers are used to help make decisions (social studies).
18. Explain how computer graphics are used as devices for gathering and processing data (social studies).
19. Describe computer applications such as information storage and retrieval, process control and aids to decision making, computation and data processing, as well as simulation and modeling (social studies).
20. Describe ways computers are used in the information and language-related careers (language).
21. Recognize the relationship of a program and input to the output.

22. Explain the basic operation of a computer system in terms of the input of data or information, the processing of data, and the output of data.
23. Recognize the need for data to be organized to be useful and relate this to its application with computers.
24. Describe how computers process data including searching, sorting, deleting, updating, summarizing and moving.
25. Describe the computer's place in our growing understanding of science.
26. Show how a scientist might use a computer.
27. Explain how computers are used in predicting, interpreting and evaluating data.
28. Explain how the computer could be used in testing and evaluating hypotheses.
29. Explain how a computer design is based on standard logic patterns.
30. State the meaning of the term "algorithm."
31. List several ways computers are used to process statistical data.

Grade: Eighth

1. Explain why data must be organized to be useful.
2. Explain the term "modeling."
3. Explain the term "robotics."
4. Differentiate between analog and digital devices.
5. Translate several mathematical relations and functions into a computer program.
6. Describe techniques computers use to process data such as searching, sorting, deleting, updating, summarizing and moving.
7. Describe several social issues that have developed due to the increase in use of computers.
8. Tell how a data base is used and how it was created.
9. In a computer context, tell how an "array" would be used.
10. Describe the difference between a one-dimensional and a two-dimensional array.
11. In a computer context, tell how "functions" would be used.
12. Identify a computer crime that might occur in your community.
13. Utilize both sound and color in creating a graphics program.

Grade: Ninth

1. List a variety of computer capabilities.
2. Discuss fields of work that are affected in an important way be the computer.
3. Using BASIC, develop a simple simulation program.
4. Using BASIC, develop a simple set of matrices.
5. Using BASIC, develop a simple set of files for a task of interest to the student.
6. Demonstrate the use of several language commands using the language Pilot.

Grade: Tenth

1. Discuss prediction, interpretation and generalization of data.
2. Discuss artificial intelligence as it is used in computing.
3. Develop an introductory level of computer literacy with the language Pascal.

Grade: Eleventh

1. Identify the elements of several computer systems.
2. Using the computer, run a program which utilizes several sampling techniques.
3. Demonstrate several statistical applications on the computer.
4. Use the language Pilot to develop a program of interest to the student.

Grade: Twelfth

1. Discuss several skills one would need to "survive and prosper" in a computer-oriented society.
2. Discuss invasion of privacy issues as they relate to computer use.
3. Use the language Pascal to develop an advanced program of interest to the student.
4. Integrate material from several data bases to make a presentation.

We hope these suggestions will inspire you to create a continuum which meets the needs of students in your school and district.

CHAPTER NINETEEN
HELPING YOURSELF TO CHANGE

In our teaching we try to present conceptual models for helping students accomplish the tasks that need attention. Hence we have a model for you to use as you begin the task of changing your behavior to use new techniques in your teaching. This approach may also be helpful for administrators as they seek to change their own and some of their teachers' attitudes and behavior. The model was developed by Edgar Schein and is found in a book entitled *The Planning of Change* by Bennis, Benne and Chin(25).

This change implementation questionnaire is based on the assumption that an individual can change her/his behavior in a systematic fashion if there is strong motivation and support from what we call our "significant other." This is the person that you turn to for advice and sympathy when you have a problem or an important decision to make. It might be your spouse or the teacher down the hall.

There are identifiable mechanisms for making change which Schein places in three categories: **Unfreezing,** or creating motivation for change; **Changing,** or developing new responses based upon new information; and **Refreezing,** or stabilizing and integrating change. Each stage results from the person's response to certain activities which can produce change.

In unfreezing, the person may move to readiness for change through a lack of confirmation of his/her previously operating self image, as, for instance, "best math teacher in the school." She/he might become ready for change through beginning to feel inadequacy or failure in her/himself. Unfreezing may also occur through the removal of self-imposed barriers which have prevented change.

Unfreezing involves an emotional or attitudinal shift which we might call "readiness to change." There are two types of attitudes which we can think of as cognitive and emotional at their source. Cognitive attitudes are not deeply ingrained and can be altered by new information. Emotional attitudes connect to our values and they are not so easily changed. If you had an anti-technology value, you probably would not have read this book. On the other hand, you may not be a technologist, but you may be willing to read the arguments for using microcomputers. If this is true, new information may allow you to change your behavior.

Change occurs when we locate information from some credible source, redefine the situation in terms we find sensible and make the decision to alter our behavior. Refreezing occurs when we integrate new responses into our personality and into significant personal relationships.

We turn now to the change implementation questionnaire which can guide you as you seek to behave in new ways to improve your teaching.

Unfreezing

In order to create a readiness for change I will:

(mark your choices in rank order based on what you feel you should do to change your behavior)
Try to analyze my behavior and see if I find some inadequacy in the area of concern.
Do my best to remove a barrier that is preventing change.
Examine what other teachers I respect are doing in order to see new possibilities.

Changing

To assist in the change process I have:

Worked to identify questionable assumptions and beliefs.
Developed new definitions of terms.
Broadened my frame of reference.
Changed my criteria for making a judgment.
Talked to my significant other about the need to change.
Developed alternatives that make sense for me.
Selected an alternative and made my decision to change.

Refreezing

The process of refreezing after change is essentially one of becoming comfortable with one's new approach to the situation. To accomplish this we need to integrate our changed behavior into our lives as new responses within our personality, as well as making them part of our important personal relationships. To assist in integrating these new behaviors I have:

Worked to see that the new behavior and attitudes are integrated in a thoughtful way with my general behavior and attitudes.

Asked my friends to help me see if my new behavior and attitudes are on target and are taking me where I want to go.

Considered unfreezing the new behaviors and attitudes so I can start over and do a better job at integrating the new and old behaviors and attitudes.

We trust this model in its present form or in an adapted form will be of assistance as you think through your position in regard to the use of microcomputers in your teaching, or for any change you are considering.

CHAPTER TWENTY
HOW MUCH ARE TEACHERS USING THE MICROS?

The Concerns-Based Adoption Model (CBAM) was developed by Gene E. Hall at the University of Texas at Austin. (26) It will allow teachers and administrators to measure how teachers feel about the new microcomputers and to find out just how much they use them.

To utilize the model it is important to bring your local practices into congruence with the several CBAM assumptions. Among these are the notions that change is a continuing process rather than an event or a decision point and that change is always made by particular individuals. Since it is individuals that actually change, the model focuses upon change as a personal experience.

Individuals, of course, change over a period of time and CBAM helps us see this progress through guiding us to analyze Stages of Concern (SOC). Our skills in using an innovation such as the microcomputer are tracked through analysis of Levels of Use (LOU).

One of the most difficult assumptions for us to meet requires the innovation to be appropriate. This is especially hard for us to manage in using microcomputers, since the courseware on the market is often programmed "page turning" that seems no different from a workbook.

CBAM further assumes that there is a formal or informal leader at the school site who serves as a "change facilitator" who assists teachers and administrators as they learn to use the innovation, in this case the microcomputer.

STAGES OF CONCERN

The concept Stages of Concern is divided into three phases. The first is concern with self where the teacher focuses upon his or her own adequacy in understanding how to go about using the microcomputer. The second phase is concern with the task of "how to do it" and issues of logistics such as getting enough micros together for a class to use them as a group. Phase three deals with the impact of the innovation. Are the students really learning more by using the computers than they were without them? These phases are in turn broken into seven stages which one can identify.

   0. Awareness: Little concern about or involvement with the innovation is indicated.

   1. Information: General awareness of the innovation and interest in learning more detail about it is indicated. The person seems to be unworried about himself/herself in relation to the innovation. S/he is interested in substantive aspects of the innovation in a selfless manner such as general characteristics, effects, and requirements for use.

   2. Personal: Individual is uncertain about the demands of the innovation, his/her inadequacy to meet those demands, and her/his role with the innovation. This includes analysis of his/her role in relation to the reward structure of the organization, decision making and consideration of potential conflicts with the existing structures or personal commitment. Financial or status implications of the program for self and colleagues may also be reflected.

   3. Management: Attention is focused on the processes and tasks of using the innovation and the best use of information and resources. Issues related to efficiency, organizing, managing, scheduling, and time demands are utmost.

   4. Consequence: Attention focuses on impact of the innovation on students in her/his immediate sphere of influence. The focus is on relevance of the innovation for students, evaluation of student outcomes, including performance and competencies, and changes needed to increase student outcomes.

5. *Collaboration:* The focus is on coordination and cooperation with others regarding use of the innovation.

6. *Refocusing:* The focus is on exploration of more universal benefits from the innovation, including possibility of major changes or replacement with a more powerful alternative. Individual has definite ideas about alternatives to the proposed or existing form of the innovation.

These general stages have been converted into a 35 item instrument titled "The Stages of Concern Questionnaire". There is also an instrument to measure Levels of Use, which is described in the next section. Both instruments and information about training for using them may be obtained from Professor Hall at the University of Texas.

Levels of Use

Stages of Concern deals with feelings of people involved in an innovation, while Levels of Use focuses upon the behaviors of individuals as they approach and use an innovation.

Levels of Use definitions are as follows:

0. Nonuse   State in which the user has little or no knowledge of the innovation, no involvement with the innovation, and is doing nothing toward becoming involved.

Decision Point A   Takes action to learn more detailed information about the innovation.

1. Orientation   State in which the user has recently acquired or is acquiring information about the innovation and/or has recently explored or is exploring its value orientation and its demands upon user and user system.

Decision Point B   Makes a decision to use the innovation by establishing a time to begin.

2. Preparation   State in which the user is preparing for first use of the innovation.

Decision Point C   Changes, if any, and use are dominated by user needs.

3. Mechanical Use   State in which the user focuses most effort on the short-term, day to day use of the innovation with little time for reflection. Changes in use are made more to meet user needs than client needs. The user is primarily engaged in a stepwise attempt to master the tasks required to use the innovation, often resulting in disjointed and superficial use.

Decision Point D-1   A routine pattern of use is established.

4. Routine   Use of the innovation is stabilized. Few, if any, changes are being made in ongoing use. Little preparation or thought is being given to improving innovation use or its consequences.

Decision Point D-2   Changes use of the innovation based on formal or informal evaluation in order to increase client outcomes.

4B. Refinement   State in which the user varies the use of the innovation to increase the impact on clients within the immediate sphere of influence. Variations are based on knowledge of both short and long term consequences for clients.

Decision Point E   Initiates changes in use of innovation based on input of and in coordination with what colleagues are doing.

5. Integration   State in which the user is combining own efforts to use the innovation with related activities of colleagues to achieve a collective impact on clients within their common sphere of influence.

Decision Point F   Begins exploring alternatives to or major modifications of the innovation presently in use.

6. Renewal   State in which the user reevaluates the quality of use of the innovation, seeks major modifications of or alternatives to present innovation to achieve increased impact on clients, examines new developments in the field, and explores new goals for self and the system.

Beginning users of microcomputers are typically at the mechanical use stage or Level 3. They are still referring to the manuals and may rely heavily on students who know more than they do. With time and continued use they will move to routine use of the technology, and they are then ready for a summative evaluation. It would be inappropriate to conduct this type of evaluation in the first year of a program since research from the University of Texas has shown that 60 to 70% of teachers are at the mechanical use stage during year one of an innovation. (27)

In introducing an innovation, the change facilitator must think systemically, that is, in terms of sub-systems such as grade levels in an elementary school or departments in a secondary school. The informal leaders of work groups are the key to facilitating change.

A number of implications arise as we seek to evaluate and analyze the impact of microcomputers. Change is a process. In order to be successful, an innovation needs implementation support; therefore, there cannot be too many innovative activities occurring at once. School innovation needs the close attention and encouragement of the principal. The principal, in turn, needs to know that the innovation is considered a priority by district staff.

School faculty need time to move from the orientation to the routine level of use as they become involved with micros. The principal must provide a stable school environment and sufficient training and resources for effective implementation. Given the parent pressures in many schools, this is not easy to achieve. Parents tend to want computer experiences for every child during the first year of operation; few districts have the resources for such rapid growth in microcomputer utilization.

When training is provided, the trainer should be perceived as an equal by the trainees. We base this statement on our experience in school districts. Individuals are more likely to allow others to guide them toward changing their attitudes if they feel the person helping them change is "like them". Our own model for carrying out inservice in districts is to locate well-liked, bright teachers and train them to be competent in the task at hand. They then serve as the trainers for their fellow teachers.

In terms of evaluation, the focus should be on the process of change in the introduction of micros and not on a given set of test scores. Summative evaluation should be delayed until the teachers to be evaluated are at the LOU Routine level. This could take several years for some staff members who grasp the new technology slowly.

It is very common in evaluation to assume that teachers are using an innovation, when, in fact, they are not. A number of teachers will resist full utilization for some time to come, even though they say they are fully using the micros. Administrators must, therefore, document the level of use carefully, using the LOU categories. If this is not done we will have studies showing "no significant difference" in outcomes where micos were used when the real story is "no significant use by staff."

We close this chapter with a form which will help you find out "How Much Are Teachers Using the Micros?"

Microcomputer Survey

Something About You...

Title/Job _____

School _____

I own a microcomputer
I use a microcomputer at work ____
I have never touched one ____
Other ____

Something About the Microcomputer in Your Life...

What do you need to know about microcomputers? (Awareness, How to Try Them Out, Technical Assistance, etc.)

What do you want to do that a microcomputer could help you do? (Computer Assisted Instruction, Computer Managed Instruction, Computer Literacy, Integrated Curriculum Planning, Organizational Operations, etc.)

What kind of help do you need regarding microcomputers? (General Information, Planning, Applications, Selection, etc.)

Can We Help You?
Name:
Address:
Phone:
Request:

With the completion of this book you are now started in what we hope will be a most satisfying exploration of microcomputers and their many uses in classrooms and schools. As we mentioned earlier, we have found a professional renewal in our use of the computer and perhaps this can be true for you, too, if you will let it happen.

As you begin to work with new forms of technology, you are joining interests with a new breed of educators who are working to prepare our young people to regain our position as a world leader in economic performance. Excellence in the use of technology appears to be a critical aspect of this effort.

FOOTNOTES

1. Rizza, Peter, *Basic Skills Evaluation* Control Data Corporation, Minneapolis, Minnesota.

2. Passman, B., Personal Communication, Sperry Univac Corporation, Blue Bell, Pennsylvania, January, 1979.

3. Magidson, E.M., " Issue Overview: Trends in Computer Assisted Instruction", *Educational Technology* 18, 4 (1978), 5-8.

4. Splittgerber, F.L., "Computer-based Instruction: A revolution In The Making?," *Educational Technology 19*, 1 (1979), 20-26.

5. Taylor, S., et al., "The Effectiveness of CAI," Annual Convention of the Association for Educational Data Systems, New York, 1974.

6. Laurillard, D.M., "The Design and Development of CAI Materials In Undergraduate Science," *Computer Graphics 2*, (1977), 241-247.

7. Ballard, Richard, *The Educational Software Market*, published by TALMIS, Oak Park, Illinois, 1981.

8. Conference Board of the Mathematical Sciences Committee on Computer Education, *Recommendations Regarding Computers in High School Education*, April, 1972.

9. Branscomb, Lewis, "Electronics and Computers: An Overview," *Science*, Vol. 215, February, 1982.

10. Moursound, David, *Precollege Computer Literacy: A personal Computing Approach*, Department of Computing and Information Science, University of Oregon, Eugene, Oregon, 1981.

11. Prepared by staff of the *Executive Educator*, based on materials developed by the Northwest Regional Education Laboratory, and published in the *Executive Educator*, March, 1982.

12. Beck, John J. Jr., "The Microcomputer Bandwagon: Is It Playing Your Tune?", *The Directive Teacher*, Winter/Spring, 1982.

13. Ross, Peter, *Introducing Logo*, Addison Wesley Publishing Co., Reading, Massachusetts, 1983.

14. Ibid.

15. Watt, Daniel, "Logo in the Schools," *Byte* Magazine, August, 1982, pp. 116-134.

16. Ibid.

17. Papert, Seymour, *Mindstorms- Children, Computers, and Powerful Ideas*, Basic Books, New York, New York, 1980.

18. Allen, Judith, et. al., MicroSIFT Survey Of Computer Using Teachers, published by the Northwest Regional Education Laboratory, Portland, Oregon.

19. Sadlier, James and Jeffery Stanton, *The Book Of Apple Computer Software: 1981*, The Book Company, Lawndale, California, 1980.

20. Naisbitt, James, *Megatrends*, Warner Books, New York, New York, 1982.

21. Shawn, Joel, "Microcomputer Infusion Model," available from the Office of the Los Angeles County Superintendent of Schools, 1983.

22. Luehrmann, Arthur, interview with Lois Coit, "What Is Computer Literacy?," *Christian Science Monitor*, April 15, 1983.

23. Moore, Barbara, "Inservice Training For Using Microcomputers," Available from Fullerton School District, Fullerton, California, 1983.

24. Givner, Bruce, "Computer Skills Continuum," available from Irvine Unified School District, Irvine, California, 1983.

25. Schein, Edgar H., "The Mechanisms of Change," *The Planning of Change* by Warren Bennis, Kenneth D. Benne and Robert Chin, published by Holt, Rinehart and Winston, Inc., New York, New York, 1969.

26. Hall, Gene E., Procedures for Adopting Educational Innovations Project, Research and Development Center for Teacher Education, University of Texas, Austin, Texas, 78712. For Levels of Use see Hall, G.E. and Loucks, S.F., "A Developmental Model for Determining Whether the Treatment is Actually Implemented", *American Educational Research Journal*, 1977, 14(3), pp. 263-276. For Stages of Concern see Hall, G.E., George, A.A., and Rutherford, W.L., "Measuring Stages of Concern About an Innovation: A Manual for use of the SoC Questionnaire," Research and Development Center for Teacher Education, The University of Texas at Austin, 1977.

GLOSSARY

Abacus   A device for performing calculations by sliding beads or counters along rods. An early (3000 BC) form of biquinary calculator.

ASCII Character Set   The most common information code, American Standard Code for Information Interchange (ASCII). It is an 8 bit code which commonly uses 7 bits; they provide 128 characters including upper case, numbers, spacing and additional punctuation.

Authoring Language   A language used by authors or programmers to prepare software for further use. Computers also use machine language on paper tape (the lowest level language) and assembly language (the middle level language).

BASIC   Beginner's All-purpose Symbolic Instruction Code. One of the simplest computer languages to learn and use in programming. Sophisticated programmer's often move on to use PASCAL after learning BASIC.

Branching   Selecting a choice from several alternatives in a software program. For example, in studying US History one could branch to period a) up to the Civil War, or period b) after the Civil War.

Computer Assisted Instruction (CAI)   An instructional approach which utilizes the computer or microcomputer as the sole means for delivering instruction. Typically the program for students is interactive, that is, the student responds to the computer and then the computer selects the next comment or question based on the student response. CAI is often designed to let the student progress at her or his own pace.

Computer Managed Instruction (CMI)   As we have indicated in the chapter on CAI, there are two different notions of computer managed instruction. The most common use sees CMI as a testing and record keeping program. CMI can also mean an approach where CAI is used part of the time, say 60%, and other media such as video tapes, film, slides, audio tapes and print materials are used 40% time. These different instructional approaches are controlled through a program that uses each strategy where, through pilot testing, it has proven to be most effective with students.

COBOL   This COmmon Business Oriented Language is designed for commercial data processing and other business uses.

Courseware   Courseware is software that is designed to deliver instruction such as the Mc Millan math series. Software not designed for instruction is called general applications software. The Word Star word processing program is an example.

Diagnostic   The aspect of instruction wherein the teacher decides what the needs of the student are. The program Typing Tutor has a diagnostic set of activities which help the student identify those letters and numbers which are typed less accurately and more slowly than others.

Digitizer   A device that converts an analog measurement, which is continuous like the hands on a clock, to a digital form, like the new clocks that just display the numbers.

Disk Drive   The little rectangular box that the diskettes go into in order to operate a microcomputer. If you have one disk drive, it has a controller in it to tell the disk drive what the computer has signaled for it to do. If you have two disk drives, one of them called Drive A has the controller and the other one, Drive B, receives commands from Drive A.

Dot (Matrix) Printer   This is the most common type of printer. It has high speed and prints character-like configurations of dots from wire ends. It is the printer needed to print out (dump) graphics. It is usually less expensive than the letter quality printer.

Drill and Practice   The most common type of courseware available because it is the easiest to program. It is very effective in teaching materials that must be memorized like multiplication tables and foreign language.

Floppy Disk   A thin little flexible platter coated with magnetic material that is used to store program materials from a microcomputer. It looks alot like a 45 RPM record.

FORTRAN   FORmula TRANslator. A so called compiler language developed by IBM to use in scientific and business programming.

Game Paddles   Sometimes referred to as game controllers, these paddles are plugged into the board inside a microcomputer. They allow the player to "hit" electronic blips and perform other functions that striking a key on the keyboard won't accomplish.

Grappler Card   A card which allows the microcomputer to print out graphics or text on a printer. The card goes in the "printer" or number 1 slot inside the microcomputer.

Hardware   The microcomputer and all of the components that go with it to make up a permanent system except the programs that are on disks. These are the software.

High Resolution   High resolution screen displays or print out (typically of graphics) refers to the conversion of signals from the computer into very clean, straight lines. Since high resolution capability costs more, it is important for the buyer to find out if he or she really needs this high quality display. Perhaps low resolution will do almost as well and save money.

Integer BASIC   Integer BASIC is a language in which one can program rapidly. It is used for programming in education, game playing and graphics. Applesoft BASIC is used for business and scientific programming.

Interactive   Courseware that is interactive requires a response from the student. For example, a program that teaches students to recognize musical notes might play a simple five note tune and then ask the student to pick one of three five note sequences that is the same as the tune.

Interface   The boundary between two parts of a system. For example, a printer interface card goes inside the microcomputer and it serves as the connecting link from the microcomputer to the printer.

Joystick   A stick or lever that can be pointed or tilted in various directions to control the cursor in game activities or other movement desired.

Koala Pad   The Koala Pad is a small graphics board that uses a stylus (or even your finger) to draw different sized lines, shapes and curves.

K (48 K)   A block of 1024 memory locations is called 1 "K" of memory. Each memory location is called a "byte" of information. A typical diskette holds 125 K of information or about 25 typewritten pages in a double-spaced format. 48 K of memory is standard for an Apple II plus and 64 K is needed to operate the word processing program Word Star. One buys a language card to obtain additional K or memory and this is then plugged into the inside of the microcomputer.

Letter Quality Printer   A printer that is bigger than a dot matrix printer, costs more, and produces a higher quality letter print out. It cannot print out graphics as the dot matrix can.

LOGO   The "turtle" langauge created by Seymour Papert at the Massachusetts Institute of Technology to help children learn to program the computer. It can be used to work with lists and arithmetic as well. It puts the child in an active rather than a passive stance in learning about a topic.

Low Resolution   The conversion of signals from the computer into displays or print out that have a low or less distinct quality than high resolution. Low resolution programs cost less than high resolution and sometimes it is more important to save the money than to have a more distinct display of the data.

Mainframe Computer   The large (time-sharing) computer used when a great deal of memory is needed as well as high speed in processing. School districts often have a mainframe to do personnel, payroll and record keeping.

Microchip   An integrated circuit residing on a single silicon chip which is capable of performing the essential functions of a computer. It can be thought of as the "computer on a chip."

Microcomputer   A small computing system consisting of hardware and software, where the processing is done through integrated circuits on silicon chips. It is typically not as costly as a minicomputer, nor does it operate as rapidly or have as much memory. The Apple II and Radio Shack are microcomputers.

Minicomputer   The middle sized computer which offers higher performance than micro-computers. The minicomputer typically has more memory and operates faster than the microcomputer. It also offers more high level languages, operating systems and networking possibilities than is true for the microcomputer.

Modem   A modem is a telephone-like device that converts information from a form which is compatible with a computer to a form which can travel in a telephone transmission and then, for example, converts it back to computer form again.

Monitor   The TV-like screen which displays the signals from the computer. Monitors offer displays in color, black and white, and green on black (the green screen).

Paddle   Synonym for game controller, that is, a device that is plugged into the board of the computer to allow the user to "hit" electronic blips and perform other functions that cannot be accomplished by striking a key on the keyboard.

PLATO   The largest collection of courseware in the world is on PLATO, which was developed at the University of Illinois. It is now owned by Control Data Corporation (CDC) and we call it Illinois-PLATO to distinguish it from Micro-PLATO, also owned by CDC. Micro-PLATO runs on several microcomputers and has not been through the extensive developmental process that Illinois-PLATO has. See Chapter 4 for further clarification.

Prescriptive   To follow the analogy used for diagnosis, the prescriptive part of a courseware program helps you improve. If you are diagnosed to need work on typing the letters "m" and "u", for example, the prescriptive part of the program might have you type "m", "n", "u" and "i" four times as fast as you can to see if you can improve your speed and accuracy. Then if you didn't improve enough you would do it again.

Software   The programs that are on diskettes for instruction and for administrative use are called software. What you would ordinarily think of as software, the manuals that go with the diskettes, are called documentation.

Strip Printer   A printer that prints out data on thin little strips of paper rather than letter sized sheets.

Terminal   An extension of a mainframe computer where the operator can type in data and also read displays coming back from the computer.

Transistor   A tiny device used in computers which is made by attaching three or more wires to a small wafer of semiconducting material. They perform the same function as the vacuum tubes did in an earlier day.

ANNOTATED BIBLIOGRAPHY

BOOKS

Abelson, Harold, *Apple Logo*, BYTE/McGraw Hill, Peterboro, New Hampshire, 1982.

> A fine collection of Logo projects using graphics and language.

Abelson, Harold, and Andrea Di Sessa, *Turtle Geometry*, The MIT Press, Cambridge, Massachusetts, 1981.

> A strong collection of advanced turtle geometry projects in mathematics and science for high school and college students.

Albrecht, Robert L., LeRoy Finkel and Jerald R. Brown, *BASIC, 2ND Edition, A Self-Teaching Guide*, John Wiley and Sons, New York, New York, 1978.

> A standard introduction to programming in BASIC that sells widely.

Archer, Doug, *Microcomputers for Special Education*, Minneapolis, Minnesota, ERIC Document Reproduction Service, ED 226718, 1980.

> A good introduction for special educators and administrators concerned with special education.

Ball, Marion and Sylvia Charp, *Be A Computer Literate!*, Creative Computing Press, Morris Plains, New Jersey, 1981.

> An introductory work aimed at the elementary teacher. Contains many illustrations and has a glossary.

Ballard, Richard, *The Educational Software Market*, published by Talmis, Oak Park, Illinois, 1981.

> Provides brief descriptions of all commercial software on the market at the time of publication.

Billings, Karen and David Moursund, *Are You Computer Literate?*, Dilithium Press, Beaverton, Oregon, 1979.

An introductory book which covers "what is a computer"?, how computers are used and the history of computers. Contains self-tests, glossary and reference list.

Dertouzos, Michael L., and Joel Moses, *The Computer Age: A Twenty Year View*, MIT Press, Cambridge, Massachusetts, 1980.

A scholarly work with sections on prospects for the individual in a computer oriented society, trends in traditional computer uses, socioeconomic effects of computers and trends in technologies underlying use of the computer.

Doerr, Christine, *Microcomputers and the 3 R's- A Guide for Teachers*, Hayden Book Company, Inc., Rochelle Park, New Jersey.

Discusses the educational possibilities for using computers. Aimed at secondary teachers and administrators. Includes many curriculum suggestions and a reference section.

Dornbusch, Sanford, and Richard Scott, *Evaluation and the Exercise of Authority*, Jossey-Bass, San Francisco, California, 1975.

A collection of evaluation studies from a dozen different types of organizations together with a basic theory of evaluation based on the studies.

Frenzel, Louis E. Jr., *The Howard W. Sams Crash Course in Microcomputers*, Howard W. Sams & Company, Indianapolis, Indiana, 1980.

A complete programmed text on using microcomputers. Good definitions and relevant self-tests.

Goldenberg, Paul, *Special Technology for Special Children*, University Park Press, Baltimore, 1979.

A helpful book on the use of computers in special education.

Guertin, Jean, and James Rudolf,*Microcomputer Planning Handbook*, Office of the Los Angeles County Superintendent of Schools, Imperial Boulevard, Downey, California, 1982.

A most helpful handbook that many school districts have utilized to good effect.

Hamblen, John W., and Carolyn P. Landis, *The Fourth Inventory of Computers in Higher Education: An Interpretive Report*, Westview Press, Boulder, Colorado, 1980.

Articles on instructional computing, administrative computing, computer centers and many other topics of interest to elementary and secondary administrators looking for new approaches by viewing higher education where computers have been in use for several decades.

Horn, Carin E., and James L. Poirot, *Computer Literacy- Problem Solving With Computers*, Sterling Swift Publishing Company, Austin, Texas, 1981.

Designed for the beginning student. Assumes the reader has no background with computers. Contains a discussion of the use of BASIC, good glossary and bibliography.

Horn, Carin E., and James L. Poirot, *Intructional Manual* to accompany the text cited above.

Manual contains chapter summaries, questions and answers, review materials and "things to do."

Larsen, Sally Greenwood, *Computers For Kids*, Apple II Plus edition, Creative Computing Press, Morristown, New Jersey, 1981.

Basic computer literacy book with large print text for young readers. Contains exercises and games as well as lesson outlines.

Moursund, David, *Precollege Computer Literacy: A Personal Computing Approach*, Department of Computing and Information Science, University of Oregon, Eugene, Oregon, 1981.

The booklet is written especially for training students and teachers to use computers in secondary schools.

Moursund, David, *Introduction to Computers in Education for Elementary and Middle School Teachers*, Department of Computing and Information Science, University of Oregon, Eugene, Oregon, 1981.

An overview of ways computers can be used in elementary and middle schools. Includes many examples as well as a computer literacy curriculum.

Naisbitt, James, *Megatrends*, Warner Communications, New York, New York, 1982.

Perhaps the most widely quoted current book dealing with the future of high technology societies.

Papert, Seymour, *Mindstorms*, Basic Books Inc., New York, New York, 1980.

The philosophical and educational foundations of Logo in a most entertaining and articulate form.

Poole, Lon, Martin McNiff and Steven Cook, *Apple II User's Guide*, OSBORNE/McGraw Hill, Berkeley, California, 1981.

Some experts find this to be the best single book on using the Apple. Contains sections on standard operating procedures, programming, advanced programming and graphics.

Poirot, James L., *Computers and Education*, Sterling Swift Publishing Company, Austin, Texas, 1980.

Covers computer literacy, software availability, applications for administration and contains a bibliography.

Rugg, Tom and Phil Feldman, *32 BASIC Programs for the Apple Computer*, Dilithium Press, Beaverton, Oregon, 1981.

Includes chapters on applications programs, educational programs, games and graphics. Good for readers who want to learn programming.

Sadlier, James, and Jeffery Stanton, *The Book of Apple Computer Software: 1981*, The Book Company, Lawndale, California, 1980.

Fine coverage on all types of software, including education. Also available in more recent editions.

Schein, Edgar H., "The Mechanisms of Change," seen in *The Planning of Change*, by Warren Bennis, Kenneth D. Benne and Robert Chin, Holt Rinehart and Winston, Inc., New York, New York, 1969.

Scholarly articles covering many aspects of the change process. Especially helpful when a school is about to introduce computers.

Sippl, Charles J., and Roger J. Sippl, *Computer Dictionary*, Howard W. Sams and Company, Indianapolis, Indiana, 1981.

Appears to be the standard in its field. The definitions are somewhat technical.

Taylor, Robert P., *The Computer In The School: Tutor, Tool, Tutee*, Teachers College Press, New York, New York, 1980.

A collection of essays in the field by pioneers Bork, Dwyer, Luehrmann, Papert and Suppes. A selected bibliography and index.

VanLoves, 1983 *Apple II/III Software Directory*, Advanced Software Technology, Inc., Overland Park, Kansas, 1982.

This is the most extensive collection of information on Apple software we know about. It is very useful and has over 200 entries in education alone.

Willis, Jerry, and Merl Miller, *Computers for Everybody*, Dilithium Press, Beaverton, Oregon, 1981.

A favorite, non-technical introduction that is widely read and used by educators.

Willis, Jerry, *Peanut Butter and Jelly Guide to Computers*, Dilithium Press, Beaverton, Oregon, 1978.

>An earlier non-technical standard that is especially good for teachers and students who are somewhat negative about technology.

ARTICLES

Alanzo, Hanna Ford, and Slone Eydie, "Microcomputers: Powerful Learning Tools With Proper Programming," *Teaching Exceptional Children*, November, 1981.

Allen, Judith, et. al., MicroSIFT Survey of Computer Using Teachers, published by the Northwest Regional Education Laboratory, Portland, Oregon.

Barnes, B.J., and Shirley Hill, "Microcomputer-Logo Before Lego/TM?," *The Computing Teacher*, May, 1983.

Beck, John J. Jr., "The Microcomputer Bandwagon: Is It Playing Your Tune?," *The Directive Teacher*, Winter/Spring, 1982.

Bennet, Randy E., "Applications of Microcomputer Technology to Special Education," *Exceptional Children*, October, 1982.

Branscomb, Lewis, "Electronics and Computers: An Overview", *Science*, Vol. 215, February, 1982.

Bruwelheide, Janis H., "Teacher Competencies for Microcomputer Use in the Classroom: A Literature Review," *Educational Technology*, October, 1982.

Givner, Bruce, "Computer Skills Continuum", available from Irvine Unified School District, Irvine, California, 1983.

Golden, Frederick, "Here Come the Microkids," *Time*, May 3, 1982.

Hall, Gene E., Procedures For Adopting Educational Innovations Project, Research and Development Center For Teacher Education, University of Texas, Austin, Texas.

Laurillard, D.M., "The Design and Development of CAI Materials in Undergraduate Science", *Computer Graphics 2*, 1977.

Luehrmann, Arthur, interview with Lois Coit, "What is Computer Literacy?", *Christian Science Monitor*, April 15, 1983.

Magidson, E.M., "Issue Overview: Trends in Computer Assisted Instruction", *Educational Technology 18*, 4, 1978.

Mazur, K., "Grow Old Along With Me: The Best is Yet to Be," *Personal Computing*, August, 1980.

Miller, Inabeth, "The Micros Are Coming," *Media and Methods*, April, 1980.

Moore, Barbara, "Inservice Training For Using Microcomputers", Available from Fullerton School District, Fullerton, California, 1983.

Shawn, Joel, "Microcomputer Infusion Model", Available from the Office of the Los Angeles County Superintendent of Schools, Los Angeles, California, 1983.

Splittgerber, F.L., "Computer-based Instruction: A Revolution in the Making", *Educational Technology 19*, 1, 1979.

Taylor, S., et. al., "The Effectiveness of CAI", Annual Convention of the Association of Educational Data Systems, New York, New York, 1974.

Tursman, Cindy, "Powerful Ideas," *Educational Leadership*, November, 1982.

SUBJECT INDEX